Pelican Books
Western Capitalism Since the War

Michael Kidron is a political economist.
He writes about capitalism: the abortive
capitalism of the South or Third World;
the over-ripe capitalism of the West; and
the state capitalism of the East. He has
travelled widely. He works at the Institute
of Commonwealth Studies, Oxford, and
at the Pakistan Institute of Development
Economics, Karachi. Michael Kidron
lives in London.

Michael Kidron

Western Capitalism Since the War Revised Edition

Penguin Books

Penguin Books Ltd, Harmondsworth,
Middlesex, England
Penguin Books Inc., 7110 Ambassador Road,
Baltimore, Maryland 21207, U.S.A.
Penguin Books Australia Ltd, Ringwood,
Victoria, Australia

First published by Weidenfeld & Nicolson 1968
Revised edition published in Pelican Books 1970
Copyright © Michael Kidron, 1968, 1970

Made and printed in Great Britain by
Hazell Watson & Viney Ltd, Aylesbury, Bucks
Set in Linotype Times

Contents

Preface to the Pelican Edition

Apart from minor improvements in style and a sprinkling of
footnotes – enclosed in square brackets – Parts 1 and 2 of this
edition have been left as first published. Part 3 is wholly new.

Lund
December 1969

Preface to the First Edition

Political economy is booming. A few writers are once again trying to see how capitalism works as a system. The interest is fairly recent and the output small. It is still far from being in the mainstream of economic thought, a position it lost a century or so ago. But it is there, likely to grow – and this essay is part of it.

The essay shares with the other contributions an impatience with national preoccupations and peculiarities except as indications of a general trend. Less happily, it shares a haphazard sense of proportion and a summary way with qualification, reservation and restraint – but this is inescapable when writing without the resources of orthodoxy. It also shares many debts, some acknowledged, to many people. Where it claims a little distinction is in its presuppositions, almost wholly implicit:

that capitalism is larger than 'the west' as normally understood, and embraces the bureaucratic state capitalisms of 'the east' as well as the arrested capitalisms of 'the south';

that western capitalism, the outgrowth of the original private enterprise model, cannot be understood except in terms of the world system, and particularly in terms of its competitive relations with state capitalism;

and – a methodological point this – that Marx's attempt to grasp the workings of the system is neither laughable nor holy. Allowance made for its primitiveness, it can be used to effect.

Only one of these – the second – needs elaboration. Except in Chapter 3, where it is stripped down to essentials, no attempt is made to place western capitalism in a context of the system as a whole. In particular, no mention is made of the west's contribution to sustaining the conservative, class-ridden state-capitalisms of 'the east', or in perpetuating the desperation of the backward world. No judgement is intended in the omissions. It is demonstrable that the malignancy of the west's intervention grafted a like malignancy on post-revolutionary Russia, the consequences of which are still embedded in Cold War. It is equally demonstrable that the societies maimed and shattered by the imperialist explosion of the last century are again being maimed and shattered – by the growing economic isolationism of the west (an imperialist implosion as it were) as well as by some of the consequences of Cold War. But so important are these demonstrations, they had best be treated separately, not as minor themes in the present essay. What is important here is to show that even under the exceptionally favourable external circumstances that have existed since the war, western capitalism is deeply unstable, as any system of conflict must be.

The essay has grown out of small beginnings not all of which are fully outgrown. That it has been able to do so is due to the critical support of Tony Godwin and Nina Kidron; to the critical criticism of Nigel Harris and a number of other friends who read the manuscript; to the generous help of my colleagues at the University of Hull; and to the patience and efficiency of the University's librarians. Except in details, the manuscript was completed in March 1967.

Chapter Three has appeared in an earlier form in the quarterly *International Socialism*, a journal in which many of the ideas presented here were first exercised.

Lund, E. Yorks.
December 1967

Introduction   The Experience

High employment, fast economic growth and stability are now considered normal in western capitalism.[1] Half the working population have known nothing else.

Unemployment has not disappeared. The American method of counting would show the current British figure of around $2\frac{1}{2}$ per cent to be a full percentage point higher; if German definitions were used it would go up another seven tenths. Unemployment is particularly harsh on some sections of the population – the unskilled, the uneducated, the old – and on the national scapegoats : Negroes in the US, immigrant workers in Europe. But it is not the problem it was before the war when ten per cent unemployment was thought low and twenty-five per cent and above not unknown. On the whole, it has been less of a problem than the shortage of labour, particularly skilled labour.

Something of the sort can be said of growth. Individual performances have been very different, and most countries have had bursts of speed and then suffered hold-ups, but the system as a whole has never grown so fast for so long as since the war – twice as fast between 1950 and 1964 as between 1913 and 1950, and nearly half as fast again as during the generation before that.[2]

Not everyone has benefited. In Britain there are still seven

1. For the purposes of this essay 'western capitalism' covers Belgium, Denmark, France, West Germany, Italy, the Netherlands, Norway, Sweden, Switzerland, the United Kingdom, Canada and the United States, the choice having been governed primarily by the availability of comparable figures.

2. Unweighted averages, based on Angus Maddison, *Economic Growth in the West*, New York: The Twentieth Century Fund, George Allen & Unwin, 1964, Tables I-1, A-2, pp. 28, 201–2; and 'How Fast Can Britain Grow?', *Lloyds Bank Review*, January 1966. Table 1, p. 2.

or eight million people living below the official subsistence minimum. In the United States two fifths of all families – a large proportion of them Negroes – live on less than the 'modest but adequate' working-class budget defined by the Bureau of Labor Statistics. And even when these poor and poorest are lost in broader categories it is still true that better living for all has not upset the traditional social pattern. In Britain where real wages have doubled since the war, their share in the national income – forty-two per cent – is still roughly what it was in 1870. Give or take a few percentage points, the same goes for the other countries – their even faster rise in living standards has made as small an impact. Yet after all the qualifications and refinements, the general point remains: economic expansion since the war has been unprecedented and with it has gone an unprecedented rise in living standards.

So too with stability. There have been very few occasions anywhere that output has actually fallen since the war, and then by no more than two per cent on an annual basis, while between the wars it was below peak in most countries for one third of the time and there were falls of up to one fifth of gross domestic product.

High employment, growth and stability explain one another to some extent. Without the immense increase that took place in labour input – it rose $3\frac{1}{2}$ times faster in the fifties than between 1913 and 1950 – and the accompanying rise in fixed investment – up by two thirds to twenty-two per cent of total output [3] – growth could have been nothing like as fast. But without rapid growth the economies could not have absorbed the additional labour and capital. Had expansion been erratic, the vast migrations from rural occupations at home and abroad would have been less likely; and so too the high rate of investment. But without them stability would have been less. And so on and on. Each can be seen as the immediate cause of the others, together forming a causal loop that can be made to revolve in any direction from any point.

3. From Maddison, *Economic Growth*, Tables I-6, G-1, G-2, III-1, pp. 36, 76, 228. Unweighted averages.

The loop itself needs to be explained. In the thirties it was one of unemployment–stagnation–instability; now it is one of high employment–growth–stability. The interconnexions and sequence are the same. Only the level is different.

Part 1 of this essay will attempt to explain the reasons for the new situation; Part 2 will look at some of the results; and Part 3 will set out the reasons for believing western capitalism will show itself to be a very unstable system in the seventies.

Part 1 *Explanations*

1. Planning

Ideology

The case for seeing government activity as the key to post-war stability is simply put. The public sector everywhere is huge. It spends anything between thirty and forty-five per cent of gross national product; it accounts for roughly the same proportions of capital spending; and employs up to a quarter of the total labour force. It can be used effectively to underpin government economic policy. More important, government policy can adjust demand to whatever level seems necessary to ensure full employment; and by direct intervention a government can also adjust the proportions between different sectors of the economy to ease existing or expected bottlenecks.

Taking the last first, there is no denying that state intervention and assistance have done much to change the face of western capitalism since the war. They have resulted in the large modernized public sectors, covering energy, transport, communications and finance, which lie at the foundation of planning in most countries. They have also affected the structure of the private sector. In Britain, the Government sweated the cotton textile industry to three fifths its 1959 size in a matter of six years; the air-frame industry was halved into two major groups at the end of the fifties and is in the process of being halved again. Shipbuilding is waiting for the distribution of £70 million in rationalization money; machine tools, computers, the docks, and more are queueing up for the attention of the new state merchant bank, the Industrial Reorganization Corporation. In Italy, the steel and oil industries are monumental evidence for the success of this type of state intervention, as are chemicals, electrical engineering and almost each of the industries and services that have sustained the 'economic miracle'. Roughly the same could be said of all western countries – through a mixture of forced rationalization and nationalization, they have done much to modernize their structure, and are continuing to do so.

It is when considering the second, less specific weapon in the state economic armoury – the adjustment of demand to secure full employment – that doubts about the effectiveness of government policy occur. Dow, in what has rapidly become the standard text in Britain, shows that stability and full employment was far from being the sole, or even the main, concern of official policy; that, 'policy ... must on the contrary be regarded as having been positively destabilizing' in every important case between 1945 and 1960.[1] For Europe as a whole, it is clear that the two widespread recessions of the fifties were as much caused as cured by official measures.[2] Nearer to our time, it took the British Government a full eighteen months until July 1966 to club business into the depressed state required by international financial and political considerations; while de Gaulle, faced with an opposite problem at that time, took as long to coax French business from its stabilization freeze, and then not too successfully. Finally, there is little evidence that the public sectors have been used consistently and effectively to even out the ups and downs of economic activity.

The economics sophisticate makes light of this sort of evidence. In the contemporary mixed economy, runs the argument, private business is confident that the state would correct any spontaneous tendency towards recession; it is assured, therefore, of emerging unscathed through the normal pay-off period of three years or so; and so willing to invest. In doing so, it sustains production, prices, full employment. After some experience of the resulting boom conditions, business 'will, in fact, become concerned with the risks of *not* investing, i.e. lack

1. J. C. R. Dow, *The Management of the British Economy 1945–1960*, Cambridge University Press, 1964, p. 384.

2. 'In the 1951–2 case there were distortions on the side of the balance of payments, but these came from a shock to the economy from the political sphere. In the 1957–8 case there was not much in the way of distortions in the economy; restraining action was taken precisely to prevent their arising to a serious degree ... the recessions followed from acts of policy ...' – Milton Gilbert, 'The Postwar Business Cycle in Western Europe', *American Economic Review*, May 1962, p. 100.

of capacity to meet expanding demand with consequent loss of market share to competitors, and rising labour costs due to inadequate investment to raise productivity and offset rising wages'.[3] In other words, the fact that business believes in the government's preparedness to intervene sets off a train of action which by and large obviates the need for such intervention. And if, on the occasions government does intervene, the job is botched, this hardly matters, for the tools it uses are too crude to cope with the fine adjustments needed. However, should the system really lurch towards recession, the correctives would match the task more evenly.

The argument is teleological. It rests on the view, shared by the established Left as well as the established Right, that the economy's course is determined by policy, that such policy stems ultimately from social and political pressures powerful and determined enough to modify the system, and that a welcome (or irksome) measure of discipline has thus been imposed in the interests of social welfare (Left) or in the furtherance of doctrine (Right). It sees the direction of economic policy as something essentially arbitrary, the state as the instrument of arbitrariness and 'democracy' the power to wield it. In its modern accent, and dealing with the established Left only, the argument is that 'the provision of state assistance to the development of countervailing power has become a major function of government – perhaps *the* major domestic function of government',[4] or, in English tones: 'the transformation of capitalism makes it indispensable that *someone* should regulate it' and 'the operative factor . . . has been the growing power of the people'.[5]

It is a persuasive view, and important because it is the political bond between Labour and Conservative parties the world over: for both, arbitrariness defines the area of politics – if regulation can have cut so deep across the grain of the system, it can as surely be pressed further (Left) or pushed back (Right), depending on the relation of forces within the conventional power structure, and on nothing else.

3. Maddison, *Economic Growth in the West*, p. 50. Emphasis added.
4. J. K. Galbraith, *American Capitalism*, Penguin edition, 1963, p. 141.
5. John Strachey, *Contemporary Capitalism*, Gollancz, 1956, pp. 279, 152.

It follows from the argument that the state would tilt most towards labour where labour was politically strongest, notably in Britain compared with the rest of western Europe; or that the great strides towards economic management would be taken when political Labour is in power, say, between 1945 and 1950 or now, in Britain; or that state planning would contribute to an enlargement of democratic control.

Not a bit of it. Official welfare payments in Britain form a smaller proportion of gross national product than in most other countries – 6·4 per cent (1960) compared with 10·4 per cent for West Germany, 9·2 for Austria, 9·1 for Sweden, 8·8 for Belgium, 8·3 for France, 7·9 for Italy, 6·8 for Denmark.[6] They form a smaller part of the average worker's take home pay – 3·5 per cent (1955) compared with 25·5 per cent in Italy, 20·5 per cent in France, or 14·3 per cent in Germany;[7] and a smaller relative charge on capital – in 1960 British employers were contributing directly twenty-one per cent of social security revenue, compared with seventy-two per cent in Italy, sixty-nine per cent in France and forty-one per cent in Germany,[8] and they were not contributing more indirectly through general business taxation than in Germany, say, or Austria. When it comes to specific welfare provisions, the British worker can only wonder how he missed out on the French worker's *legal* right to three weeks' annual holiday with pay (as opposed to his own customary but unenforceable fortnight); or the one month's notice or payment *in lieu* after six months at work (compared to his own single week's notice or pay); or the way many workers in most European countries can lay some legal claim to their job; or the German workers' inflation-proof retirement pension at three quarters of average earnings during their last three years of employment; or the level of family allowances – between twice

6. 'Social Security in Britain and Certain Other Countries', *National Institute Economic Review*, No. 33, August 1965, Table 6, p. 56.

7. I.L.O. *Labour Costs in European Industry*, I L O Studies and Reports, New Series No. 52, Geneva, 1959, Table 13, pp. 52–3.

8. G. L. Reid, 'Supplementary Labour Costs in Europe and Britain' in G. L. Reid and D. J. Robertson (eds.) *Fringe Benefits, Labour Costs and Social Security*, George Allen & Unwin, 1965, Table 32, p. 101.

and six times higher in the major west European countries than in Britain. Even the much vaunted Health Service is scarcely what it was and certainly nothing like what it was intended to be. Squeezed by the private drug firms and starved of money by the state, it is demonstrably inadequate in every one of its services, and very near breakdown in some, as can be seen in the luxuriant growth of private, personal, and industrial health insurance schemes, the three largest of which multiplied their membership thirteen times between 1948 and 1965.[9]

As for the supposed conjunction of Labour government and planning, nothing could be further from the facts. On the first post-war occasion in Britain no provision was made for long-term forecasting and management, nor, as an American observer reported, with some surprise, was there any 'evidence of the existence of a national physical plan even for those sectors of the economy which are more or less subject to direct fiscal control'.[10] During the second period of Labour rule, the approach to systematic state intervention – setting up the Department of Economic Affairs (1964), publication of the *National Plan* (1965) – came only *after* the Conservatives had assembled the administrative machinery in the Treasury (1961 and 1962), at the National Economic Development Council (1962) and produced the first official exercise, the White Paper on *Public Expenditure in 1963–4 and 1967–8*.[11] It was an approach, besides, that faltered at the first sign of economic difficulties. Far from state planning being a product of social democracy's attempt to recast society and the economy in a different mould, the deepest commitment to it and the most long-lived (since 1946) has been the French Government's no matter what shade of black has been featured on its current political banner.

Nor has planning resulted in an enlargement of popular control over the economy. Shonfield, its current historian had

9. Patrick Wood, *The Times*, 15 June 1966; Arthur Seldon, 'Which Way to Welfare?' *Lloyds Bank Review*, October 1966, p. 45.
10. Robert A. Brady, *Crisis in Britain*, Cambridge University Press, 1950, p. 517.
11. Cmnd 2235, 1963.

this to say of the recent British effort: 'It is ... a matter for concern when the new corporatist organizations by-pass the ordinary democratic process – neither throwing their own deliberations open to the public nor subjecting the bargains struck between the main centres of economic power to regular parliamentary scrutiny.'[12]

But if 'democracy' or popular pressure is no explanation for the size and variety of state economic intervention (however it might have influenced this or that particular), nor – with the same proviso – is direct business pressure.

This might seem surprising in view of the evidence of affinity in interest and personnel between business and the state. In Britain, 'the situation is quite clear: the intermixing between outsiders and the civil servants has now reached a point where the distinction between "administrative decisions" and "decisions taken by private individuals" is more and more difficult and more useless to make.'[13] In the US, 'no sharp line separates government from the private firm ... Each organization is important to the other; members are intermingled in daily work; each organization comes to accept the other's goals; each adapts the goals of the other to its own. Each organization, accordingly, is an extension of the other'.[14] In France, 'the development of ... planning in the 1950s can be viewed as an act of voluntary collusion between senior civil servants and the senior managers of big business',[15] and *pantouflage* – the interchange of civil servants and business executives for short periods – is well entrenched. In Germany, the collusion has been even greater – until very recently planning of a sort was very much a private matter conducted by the big three private banks. And so it is in every country – the public domain is policed by private gamekeepers.

Yet, all is not quite what it seems. Beyond the obvious interest

12. Andrew Shonfield, *Modern Capitalism*, Oxford University Press for The Royal Institute of International Affairs, 1965, p. 161.

13. Jean Blondel, *Voters, Parties and Leaders*, Penguin, 1965, p. 224.

14. J. K. Galbraith, *The New Industrial State*, Hamish Hamilton, 1967, p. 314.

15. Shonfield, op. cit., p. 128.

that business has in the State-as-pork-barrel and the State-as-planner, both of which are positive inducements to get as close to it as possible, there is a real fear of the *general* powers of government – the state is so much bigger and richer in resources than even the mightiest private firms. In practice individual capitals will oppose any extension of government power that is not deemed to be of direct benefit to themselves. A recent witness is Sir Paul Chambers, then Chairman of ICI, and as such no small beneficiary of government intervention. After informing shareholders of the extent to which his firm cooperates with the British Government and how willing it was to have thirty or forty senior men on government committees, he continued: 'On the other hand, your Directors would regard the giving of assistance to the government in schemes for the further control of sections of British industry, whether by nationalization or by some other means, as inconsistent with their duties to their stockholders.' [16]

It is this general mistrust that has prevented the very considerable inter-business planning in the US from evolving into state planning; that inhibited the Conservatives in Britain from bringing their planning initiatives to fruition; or that persuaded the German Government until early 1967 both to conceal its firm economic control behind the cavernous platitudes of *laissez-faire* phraseology and to devolve much of the day-to-day management to the three big banks. To put the point negatively, it is only because the number of big firms in France was small enough for their particular interest to overlap extensively with the general interests of French big capital, that planning was so easily accepted and has been so long-lived. As Shonfield writes of the *Commissariat du Plan*: 'These men talk among themselves in a kind of shorthand about the "80–20 ratio". This expresses their view that to make effective planning possible the distribution of output in industry ought preferably to be such that something close to eighty per cent of production comes from about twenty per cent of the firms.' [17] So while it is true, as Galbraith says, that 'the shortcomings of the large corpora-

16. *The Times*, 1 April 1966.
17. Shonfield, op. cit., p. 138.

tion, as a planning instrument, define the role of the modern state in economic policy',[18] the state normally assumes this role despite business and to the accompaniment of a great drumming of corporation heels.

It is difficult not to conclude that the state's growth in size and economic effect has not been a *direct* result of pressure from either business or labour. While organized labour has, on balance, favoured state involvement and capital opposed it, nothing suggests that either attitude has had much effect on the actual course of events since the war. On the contrary, the state's growth has been in a series of disjointed steps that bear every sign of *not* representing a coherent attitude working itself out in institutional form, but rather a series of *ad hoc* responses to short-term problems which could not be dealt with in any other way. Since the problems were shared more or less by all western capitalist countries and their institutional arrangements were similar at the outset, it is not surprising that they adopted similar approaches and went through a similar course.

Origins

The first post-war problem in western Europe was to repair the devastation. There had been enormous physical destruction throughout the Continent and little net investment in Britain. At the same time, there had been such an advance in industrial techniques and products during the war, especially in North America, that merely to revert to pre-war patterns would have left Europe at the mercy of the US in traditional economic terms, and of the new Russian giant in military ones. It was particularly important – and expensive – to modernize the basic transport and energy services on which recovery depended (and which had featured in pre-war debates on public ownership), and to coordinate them nationally. These provided the first post-war wave of nationalizations: in Britain, coal, gas, electricity, railways, air transport and the Bank of England were

18. 'The Role of the State', fourth 1966 BBC Reith Lecture, *Listener*, 8 December 1966, p. 842.

all taken over by 1948; in France, where the list was longer by the addition of insurance and a large part of commercial banking, the process was completed two years earlier; in Austria, the legal framework for nationalizing coal, steel, the banks and much else was completed by 1947; in Italy the need to catch up provided belated impetus to the state-run ENI (*Ente Nazionale Idrocarburi*, founded in 1953) without whose cheap fuel the phenomenal growth of private industry since then would probably not have taken place.

A subsidiary wave was the nationalization of abandoned 'collaborators'' or 'war criminals'' property. This brought Renault, the largest car firm, and Gnôme-Rhône, the largest air-engine producer, into the state's hands in France: Volkswagen in Germany; the major chemical, vehicle- and machine-building, and electrical engineering units in Austria. In Italy, it meant that the vast IRI (*Instituto per la Reconstruzione Industriale*) was taken over intact from the Fascist régime and added to, so that now it accounts for somewhere between 10 and 15 per cent of total industrial output. Parallel to nationalization went a spate of welfare legislation, concerned with concentrating uncoordinated schemes into state hands, and aimed at stemming the Left tide of the immediate post-war period. Significantly, most of it was foreshadowed during the war, as part *quid pro quo* for mass support. As Quintin Hogg put it to the House of Commons, early in 1943,

if you do not give the people reform, they are going to give you social revolution. Let anyone consider the possibility of a series of dangerous industrial strikes, following the present hostilities, and the effect it would have on our industrial recovery . . .[19]

By the fifties the early wave had spent itself. Vast investments which private capital was unable or unwilling to make were being undertaken by governments in social and physical infrastructures, and to some extent in industry. At the same time the economies had recovered, and new problems were emerging. The very size of the state sectors demanded some coherence

19. Debate on the Beveridge Report, 17 February 1943, quoted in Nigel Harris, 'The Decline of Welfare', *International Socialism* 7, Winter 1961.

in the governments' view of economic developments: freezing hundreds of millions of pounds in rationalizing British coal-mining or railways, for example, could only be justified in terms of a demand for fuel or traffic projected well in advance. In the event, the necessary exercises were undertaken so half-heartedly that they were bound to fail and the programmes needed to be substantially revamped: in the last few years alone, the British coal industry has had £400 million written off (1965); half the rail track mileage has been condemned (1963); the nationalized airways have had £110 million written off. Nor was there any way of avoiding repetitions without con-ducting a more comprehensive planning operation. This slowly sunk in during the fifties.

It was not only in the state sector that size demanded planning. The rapid growth of immense private groupings has paradoxically had the same effect. Only the largest firms can afford the techniques of modern production and research or commit resources for years in advance and still have enough in hand to respond quickly to fast-changing circumstances; or straddle a range of activities and countries wide enough to provide insurance against calamity in any one; or contain the variety of experience to sponsor organizational and technical advance. Only the largest can moderate change to suit their own convenience, or afford the loss of capital and skills that goes with the failure to do so. And only the largest can meet the largest in an increasingly open and integrated international market.

Naturally it is they that grow fastest and have everywhere become critically important in the national economy. In the United States, the five top industrial corporations held one eighth of all manufacturing assets in 1962; the fifty largest, over one third; the top 500, well over two thirds. Four com-panies were responsible for more than a fifth of all research expenditure in 1960; 400 companies for nine tenths. Forty-five firms accounted for three fifths of direct foreign investment in 1957; 300 for nine tenths. And where the 100 biggest corpora-tions held forty-four per cent of fixed assets in manufacturing in 1929, by 1962 the proportion had risen to 58 per cent. In

Britain, 180 firms employing one third of the labour force in manufacturing accounted for one half of net capital expenditure in 1963; seventy-four of these, with 10,000 or more workers each, for two fifths. Two hundred firms produce half manufacturing exports; a dozen as much as a fifth. So it is in Germany where the hundred biggest firms were responsible for nearly two fifths of industrial turnover, employed one third of the labour force and shipped one half of manufacturing exports in 1960; and where the top fifty had increased their share of sales to 29 per cent from under 18 per cent in 1954. And so it is almost everywhere, the only major exception being France, the traditional home of small units; but even there mergers are changing the scene fast.

These giants are independent, and the more powerful because of it. In most countries they provide directly out of profits between 70 and 80 per cent of the funds they use; in some industries, oil for example, between 95 and 100 per cent; sometimes, especially in Britain and the US, they are net lenders to the rest of the economy. They conduct their own research and development; their products have each a fairly distinct market; and they are highly mobile internationally. To a degree that is wholly new in capitalism they are immune from outside pressure, whether from banks or governments. And this they know. 'It would be wrong to say that Budgets are of no interest,' Lord Fleck of ICI told the (Radcliffe) Committee on the Working of the Monetary System in 1959, 'but I cannot recall any of them that made any significant change in our approach to what we were thinking of doing'; and Lords Godber of Shell and Heyworth of Unilever gave evidence in much the same vein. And in the US, only one in eight of the firms asked to curtail their spending abroad in 1964, actually did so – and then by not very much.

Relatively free of external constraints, they can pursue growth purposefully. They do this as a normal consequence of their steady and high rate of re-investment. They also do it through merger and takeover, which have been on a sharply rising curve since the war, more than quadrupling in annual value during the fifties in Britain, and quadrupling again during the first half of the sixties; doubling in number in Sweden during the same five years; reaching a crescendo in France in 1966 (two years before the final disappearance of Common Market internal tariffs) when 1,600 regroupings, amongst them true giants in steel, aluminium and vehicles, took place in the first eight months compared with 450 in the whole of 1957; and in Italy, with the formation of the gigantic Montedison, amongst others. They also do it by carrying these processes of accretion and absorption into other product markets – diversification – and other countries – by becoming 'multinational'; by spending more and more on advertising – most of the £600 million total outlay in Britain in 1965 ($20 billion in the US) and growing twice as fast as national income; and by bending the vast sums they spend under the head of research and development towards product differentiation rather than product design.

Size, diversity, long production cycles and international spread bring problems of internal coordination that need sophisticated treatment – planning in fact. Some of the handful of writers who have tried to seize capitalism as a whole – Galbraith in his *New Industrial State*, for example, or Shonfield in *Modern Capitalism* – have gone as far as to see in planning the system's 'most characteristic expression', and in the big corporation its most significant exponent. There is no need to go that far; but there is no denying that systematic business planning is both very important and very recent. By the early sixties, nine tenths of the firms responsible for one half of US factory investments were undertaking four-year projections of their activities. These are the large firms, yet even amongst these a majority – about three fifths – had done nothing at all on these lines in the late forties. Increasingly, they are shifting 'from the conventional financial framework for analysing a company's policy and operations to their analysis in terms of the flow of physical resources – raw materials, equipment, buildings, manpower'.[20] In Europe the trend is even more recent but, partly through American example and competition, it is catching on fast.

20. Shonfield, op. cit., p. 349.

Planning is not easy, not even for the biggest. One element in particular is intractable – labour. It has a will of its own and more or less independent organizations. It can, and does, take advantage of its own scarcity. Its behaviour, and therefore cost, is fundamentally unpredictable. Yet the big corporation has not given up. It cannot. As is shown more fully in the last chapter, it has taken to long-term wage contracts complete with regular, determinate wages rises or 'improvement factors'; it has done something to shift labour costs from the conflict-charged wage packet to more neutral fringe benefits; it has widened the area of agreement for increasingly narrow local bargaining; it has located new plants where labour is weakest. None of this has exorcized labour's independence. Some of it has created new threats to the determinacy of wage costs which the big corporations cannot handle at all. For this reason alone, big capital would need to rely for its continued operation on the state and state planning. The same is more or less true of their relations *inter se*. Their great relative size and independence means that their activities and plans are vitally significant to one another. A single, local compromise in wage bargaining can quickly spread; a detail of financing can have disproportionate consequences – as when ICI's loan issue in London in September 1966 triggered off bankruptcy for the Lebanon's biggest bank. Single decisions over investments have changed whole industries out of recognition (chemicals are important here) and precipitated international payment crises (oil companies feature largely here). The big firms need to take account of these factors in their own planning, to know more about each other's intentions than can be gained from even the most ambitious industrial espionage operation. Increasingly they need to relate their own plans to a shared, general framework.

Given the long production cycles in some key industries – it takes a decade or more to produce a nuclear power station or a new piece of military equipment; up to four years for a product as rehearsed and conventional as a 'new' motor car; and as much as eighteen months, if the US motor manufacturers are to be believed, to effect a small part of the marginal safety modifications newly required by Federal law – that general framework must be durable. It must be, in the words of Sir Paul Chambers, then Chairman of ICI, 'a sound, long-term, and comprehensive economic policy which the whole of industry, workers and management alike, can be reasonably confident will be adhered to by the Government or a succession of Governments'.

Given the explosive nature of their growth and the danger from massive and impotent confrontations between them at home, the framework also needs to allow for the adjustment of firms' relative sizes. This has been happening since the war as government-engineered amalgamations spread simultaneously with the hardening of anti-monopoly legislation (new anti-monopoly measures having been enacted since 1951 in Austria, Belgium, Britain, Denmark, France, Germany, Norway, Sweden and Switzerland, as well as for the Common Market and the European Coal and Steel Community as such).

Size in both the private and public sectors has invoked planning in yet another way. End users are sometimes so large, and the products they require so complex and costly, that many of these have ceased to be commodities in the true sense of goods produced for an unknown buyer, and have turned into utilities or goods made to a known buyer's specifications. In Marx's terminology, where the distinction is clearer because it is crucial to his analysis, they have changed from values to use-values. This is clearly the case with most war goods, where the state as purchaser takes the major initiative, where specifications derive from desired performance, and output, methods and everything else follow from there. Indeed the arms sector as a whole is more easily conceived in terms of economic logistics than in those of production for markets. Significantly, in so far as planning exists in the US it dates from 'the beginning of the "Sputnik" era',[21] and its most sophisticated practitioner is the Department of Defense whose methods have long since abandoned any pretence at tendering on large contracts in favour of strict physical controls over quality and quantities. Though this is less true of the private sector, the adman's jargon

21. *Goals Setting and Comprehensive Planning*, American Bureau of the Budget, 1963, p. ii, quoted in Shonfield, op. cit., p. 346n.

whereby GEC or any other firm conceives itself 'to be essentially a marketing rather than a production organization' in which 'marketing needs reach back and dictate the arrangement and grouping of production facilities'[22] conceals more than a shadow of production for predetermined use – or planning.

All of this – the size and efficiency of the state sector, the relations between big capitals, the regard for detail in performance, the need to control labour – would matter less were it not vital for economic growth, and were growth itself not considered so important. But it is. Growth has become the substance of modern macro-economics, the conventional virtue, the key to national pride as measured in international league tables. It is the declared aim of government economic measures, and the justification for official indecency: if pensioners were ignored in Britain's *National Plan*, it is because 'an income guarantee would not contribute towards faster economic growth';[23] if napalm is blessed – literally – it is ultimately because it figures in the growth of the US gross national product. Growth has even succeeded in ousting restrictiveness in the demonology of the Left. Before the war, a socialist's library in Britain was incomplete without titles like *The Problem of the Distressed Areas* or *Ten Lean Years* or *The Town that Was Murdered* or *The Means to Full Employment* – some of the better known in the Left Book Club list. Today it is inconceivable without *The Affluent Society* and its chapter on 'The Paramount Position of Production' in which Galbraith upbraids the conventional view of production as a good thing for being 'buttressed by a highly dubious but widely accepted ... interpretation of national interest; and by powerful vested interests'.[24]

The big corporations have particular reasons for pressing growth policies on their governments. Increasingly, their opera-

22. Dexter M. Keezer and associates, *New Forces in American Business*, p. 97, quoted in Paul A. Baran and Paul M. Sweezy, *Monopoly Capital*, Monthly Review Press, 1966, p. 130.

23. *The National Plan*, HMSO, 1965, Cmnd 2764, p. 204.

24. J. K. Galbraith, *The Affluent Society*, Penguin, 1962, p. 109.

tions are international in scope, and their entry into foreign markets conditional on reciprocal liberalism at home. This would be difficult in the absence of rising domestic demand. Increasingly their ability to maintain competitiveness rests on freedom to shift resources across frontiers, which demands a fairly healthy balance of payments in the home country, which in turn depends on good growth performance from the economy as a whole. Again, their competitiveness increasingly depends on a massive, open-ended commitment to research and development, well beyond the resources of the mightiest corporation; and beyond that on an educational substructure which no private firm could dream of duplicating. And since new techniques are easier to introduce when production is expanding and workers confident that their jobs will hold, and big business is increasingly organized around a constant stream of such new techniques with all that that means in organizational upheaval and uncertainty, their commitment to overall economic growth on a scale that only a government can begin to tackle is pretty strong.

Their need for sustained growth would be less imperative were it not for the growing interdependence of the developed countries, and the indeterminate nature of this interdependence. It might take the form, as in part of western Europe, of tentative integration; it might take one of 'mutual watchfulness and sensitivity to security' as, say, between East and West.[25] It might be anything in between. Whichever the case, the fact that the final authority in economic matters is dispersed over a number of independent governments, each important enough for its decisions to be crucial to those of all the others yet each taking its decisions independently and privately, and so with inherently unforeseeable consequences, makes for extreme vulnerability of each to all and for consistent attempts to offset

25. 'The closer interdependence between, say, the United States and the USSR than that between this country and some distant developed non-Communist nation (like Australia), or than that between the United States and Czarist Russia before the First World War, is a phenomenon too obvious to need stressing even though the dependence is one of mutual watchfulness and sensitivity to security' – Simon Kuznets, *Postwar Economic Growth*, Harvard University Press, 1964, p. 26.

that vulnerability by speeding up national responses to international economic events, that is by planning and centralizing economic control in each national centre.

It is easy to pinpoint when the external stimulus to planning came in Britain. While sympathy for the idea had been mounting in the Treasury and in business circles over a decade during which stop-gap measures had failed to improve the external payments position, it was the negotiations on entry to the Common Market that finally nudged the Tories into making moves in that direction. Labour's own *National Plan* identified the pinch baldly: 'The most serious economic problem facing us at the present time,' runs the Preface, 'is the balance of payments'; and the *Plan* itself begins: 'This is a plan to provide the basis for greater economic growth. An essential part of the Plan is a solution to Britain's balance of payments problem.'[26] In other countries the dangers of running a relatively open economy at full stretch have demanded less exclusive attention, but nowhere were they either negligible or neglected. Shonfield attests to the general experience. 'To begin with', he writes:

... planning was seized upon as a device for dealing with some specific problem – overcoming past neglect of certain industries or catching up with other countries or helping to smooth out fluctuations in business and employment. Only later did they come to see the relevance of what they were doing to the whole range of economic policy issues. Some of the original motives are still very pertinent. Thus, for all the contemporary feeling of greater security in the economic environment, there are also new forces making for incredible instability in the post-war world. Outstanding among them are ... the acceleration of technological change and the removal of barriers to international trade. Both of these make for sudden jolts. Planning is seen as a means of making them less sudden.[27]

In more restrained tones, as befits an international civil servant, M. Pierre-Paul Schweitzer: 'the setting of economic policy formation, particularly in the major industrial countries,

26. *The National Plan*, HMSO, 1965, pp. iii, 1.
27. Shonfield, op. cit., p. 230.

has been profoundly affected in recent years by the greater international integration of national economies'.[28]

Perhaps more convincing than anything else has been the timing of explicit commitments to planning. Almost everywhere it followed the lurch towards western currency convertibility that took place towards the end of the fifties; mostly it occurred within five years. In Britain, as has been shown, the approach was made in stages between 1961 and 1965; in Sweden, it dates from the formation of the Economic Planning Council 1962; in Holland, from 1963 when the Central Planning Bureau first embarked on a series of five-year forecasts; in Italy, where a plan (the 'Pieraccini Plan') was first published early in 1967, the preparations date from the formation of the Planning Commission following the La Malfa Report of 1962. In Germany, despite the camouflage of anti-planning propaganda, the first approach came early in 1963 with the publication of a *Report on Economic Trends in 1962 and Prospects for 1963*, and has since been taken very much further under the Grand Coalition's new 'economic policy of aggregate control'. In the US, while no formal commitment has been made, James Tobin's recommendation to President Kennedy, Summer 1962, that 'flexible planning' be adopted showed which way the wind was blowing. Even in France, the Fifth Plan (1966–70) marked a break from production targetting for particular industries which was what the planners were engaged on up till then, and the adoption of 'structural objectives'.

Planning breeds planning. A product of international integration and competition, it destroys the automatism of international adjustment – traditionally pure in theory, less so but still there in practice – and the world market becomes an increasingly unstable environment, demanding faster national adjustment, increasing national articulation and so more planning. The distinction grows sharper between the national

28. Pierre-Paul Schweitzer, Managing Director of the International Monetary Fund, 'International Aspects of the Full Employment Economy'. Address before the Trustees of the Committee for Economic Development, Los Angeles, California, 19 May 1966, Supplement to *International Financial News Service*, 20 May 1966.

economy in which competition is heteronomous, one method of attaining goals set by international competition, and the international economy where primordial competition still holds.

Naturally attempts are made to order the international environment. The wilful or inexpert use of the policy discretion now available to each government is potentially so dangerous to the rest that intense diplomatic pressure – backed by the threat of financial and political sanctions – is brought to bear to adopt particular, precisely defined policies. In Britain's case, the clearest and the most important to date, the Government was baled out of a balance-of-payments crisis at the end of 1964 on the understanding that wages would be pinned under an 'incomes policy'. In September the following year more credits were raised as the Government prepared to introduce a Prices and Incomes Bill. The following summer further loans were canvassed but now the Government was forced to impose a full-scale deflationary wage-freeze on an already faltering economy. And in November 1967, international financial aid was made contingent on devaluation of the pound together with further and savage deflation.[29] But if Britain's has been the most important, it has not been the only, case. Almost every western economy has been made to adopt specific measures to align with the rest. Working Party III of the Organization for Economic Cooperation and Development exists precisely to carry out such 'multilateral surveillance'. Nonetheless, as will be shown in a moment, voluntary international collaboration is as far away as ever.

The situation is not unlike oligopolistic competition as described in economic textbooks. Here too the behaviour of each unit (or economy) is directly determined as much by its competitors' behaviour as by its customers'; here too there is a lack of necessary information because part of it 'can be

29. [International constraints on British economic policy have since grown even tighter. Two further drafts on international credit – June 1968 and May 1969 – have been accompanied by further deflationary measures, further legislation directed against labour, and explicit undertakings by the Government – in its Letters of Intent to the International Monetary Fund and in other ways – that it will adopt and maintain internationally-agreed, domestic economic policy measures].

obtained only by observing the behaviour of persons in a range in which their behaviour depends on the assumed behaviour of others and in which the actual behaviour of the others depends on the assumed behaviour of the first group'. Here too, 'failure to develop established patterns of behaviour ... [results] in a process in which the various firms [read governments] would be trying to force each other into accepting some pattern of behaviour ... [This] warfare creates a great deal of instability, and ... does not tend to lead to a socially desirable allocation of resources'. And the failure is itself 'a consequence of the fact that the different possible agreements or quasi-agreements divide the aggregate gains in different proportions'. Writing soon after the close of the Second World War, it is not surprising that Fellner, from whom these passages are quoted, broke out of a strictly economic analysis: 'The danger of persistent misjudgement and of stalemates is greater in strongly dynamic societies with changing standards. It is greater for disputes arising in the "world society" of nations than for disputes arising in national communities, because the standards of the world society are especially vague and especially unstable.'[30]

The analogy can be carried farther (as it has been in games theory for military strategy):

... each firm knows that the others have different appraisals and that they are *mutually* ignorant about what precisely the rivals' appraisal is. Consequently, no firm can be *sure* whether the move of a rival is towards a profit-maximizing quasi-agreement or towards aggressive competition; and no firm can be sure how its own move will be interpreted. ... Even where leadership exists, the leader's moves may be misinterpreted as aiming at a change in relative positions rather than as being undertaken in accordance with the quasi-agreement.[31]

Finally, the difficulty competing oligopolists have in reaching an agreement or an understanding ('quasi-agreement') 'may

30. William Fellner, *Competition Among the Few*, Alfred A. Knopf, 1949, pp. 32–3. Earlier quotations are from pp. 14, 16, 27.
31. ibid., p. 179.

be interpreted as consequences of the fact that, while the relative strength is known to change, the changes are unpredictable. They cannot be discounted in advance. It is not advisable to disarm in relation to one's rivals. The potentiality of struggle is always present'.[32]

Limitations

Oligopolistic competition between whole economies is an alarming prospect, particularly when an increasing number of them are armed with nuclear weapons. Yet the analogy is not far-fetched. It holds in general for the relations between the blocs on either side of the Cold War split, and in particular for their 'leaders', Russia and America, with their 'hot lines', their bluff and counter-bluff, their spy networks, their competition in everything short of hurling ICBMs at each other (this being the international equivalent of the 'cut-throat' stage). It need hardly be said that the Russian plans derived from the need to survive in such an environment – more so than from the intentions of the Bolsheviks who did little in this sphere for twelve years after the Revolution – and as we have seen, rudimentary American planning, while younger, is rooted in similar soil.

The analogy holds too for each bloc in isolation. This is not the place to describe the enduring chaos of East European economic relations, the hard drive towards national autarchy in the fifties, and the painfully slow progress towards the most unambitious economic coordination through Comecon since. The results in terms of international planning are negligible and promise to remain so. As for the countries with which this essay is concerned there is no lack of material to illustrate the thesis.

NATO is a simple case. Even before de Gaulle's break in 1966, the common interest, seemingly so strong, had not managed to internationalize as little as five per cent of weapons production. There have been almost no agreements on a common need for particular weapons systems – the basic requirement – and none even on common specifications for agreed

32. ibid., p. 199.

weapons. In particular cases, Britain has been denied US satellite technology on strategic grounds, France – until she took steps to build them independently – has been denied big US computers on the same grounds, and Germany has been deprived of nuclear technology.

International monetary reform – the adaptation of the payments framework for (western) international trade to current economic realities – is a more complex case but essentially similar. Since 1957 when the US moved into deficit in her international accounts, the major western countries have been at sixes and sevens on the issue. The US, with Britain in tow, has tried on the whole to continue the present system in which the rest use dollars and pounds to settle their accounts and in which, in consequence, they are forced to hold them as reserves. The arrangement suits the 'Anglo-Saxons' well: every dollar or pound held abroad in this way, even if re-lent in the New York or London money markets, means that a similar amount of imports need not be met by exports – the rest of the world simply finances their trade gap. It means above all that the rest are financing cheaply the invasion of their home markets by the technologically more advanced 'Anglo-Saxon', overwhelmingly American, capital. The arrangement hardly suits them. Led by France, they have tried to demote the 'reserve currencies', replacing them with gold or, when this failed, with a composite reserve unit embracing a number of national currencies and more or less under their control, and latterly, when that failed, with a restricted and highly-controlled form of extended IMF drawing rights.

The details of the intellectual and political tussles are unimportant. What is, is that the battle over international currency arrangements has waxed so fierce, with the Continental Central Banks on the one hand converting their dollars into gold to the extent of half their holdings in Germany in two and a half years from 1964, or two fifths in France, and with the US and Britain on the other trying to stanch their balance-of-payments deficits, that world reserves actually fell for periods in 1965, 1966 and 1967, and are declining rapidly as a proportion of world imports, that newly-mined gold is disappearing almost entirely into private hoards and the expansion of world trade is increasingly dependent on temporary, *ad hoc* financial expedients. Were it not for a substantial increase in US expenditure abroad since 1965 in pursuit of the Vietnam war, and the phenomenal growth in the network of 'US swap-credits', a form of US-initiated bilateral mutual currency insurance which has added some $5 billion to total liquid reserves (1967), the world might well have been in the throes of a serious financial crisis.[33]

There have, of course, been rushes of international financial aid when one or other currency sagged dangerously. Britain's, the weakest, has received a mounting volume of reserve transfusions – $1,300 million in 1956, $2,000 million in 1961, $4,000 in 1964, more than $7,000 million in 1967. The network of swap arrangements and short-term financial insurance that has grown up has been used widely and with increasing frequency. But *agreement* is as distant as ever : the 'Anglo-Saxons' through their Gallic manager at the IMF, M. Pierre-Paul Schweitzer, continue to insist that 'the creation of international liquidity . . . should become a matter of deliberate decision' and to believe that that decision should be mainly theirs; the 'Europeans' insist that their fingers should be on the ledger, or failing that, that the relations between economies be projected on to gold or some other 'objective' system in order to obviate the need for continuing agreement. Meanwhile, interest rate wars alternate with interest rate disarmament in the international financial area; and France escalates its attacks on the dollar's pre-eminence.

Something of the sort can be seen even in the Common Market. Until 1967, when agreement was reached on fusion, each of the Communities in turn had been humiliated by the national governments: the High Authority of the Coal and Steel Community during the coal crisis of 1958, so that it has

33. [Between the time of first publication and mid-1969, four major international financial crises have occurred: the $3 billion rush into gold of February–March 1968, the $1·5 billion flight from the French Franc in May–June 1968, and the two stampedes into Deutsche Marks of November 1968 ($1·8 billion) and May 1969 ($4 billion).]

not since dared to use its considerable powers unless assured of unanimity from its member states; the EEC in 1965-6 over the role of the Commission itself; the Euratom Commission increasingly since the early sixties as its resources have been drained to sustain increasingly elaborate national programmes. Fundamental agreements – on transport, foreign trade, company law, customs procedure, and many more – have eluded the member governments for years, so that despite the agreement on agriculture which has contributed to lifting perhaps fifteen per cent of their joint national income on to a supranational plane, despite the Market's small scope and despite the member countries' strong common interest in facing competition from outside, there is still no more than an even chance that unity will override the pulls of nationalism. It might well be less than even, for if the principle of *le juste retour* is allowed to spread from Euratom to agriculture as it is threatening to do, with member countries becoming entitled to benefits equal to their contributions, supranationality will have sustained an irreparable shock.

It need hardly be said that each country does not operate in isolation, and that they do not shun alliances and alignments. On the contrary, as in any oligopolistic situation, these forms of action, like competition itself, are of the system's essence. What the examples attempt to show is that the basis of the alliances and grouping is self-interest as determined by national policymaking and not by outside centres of control; and that in consequence national planning is as much flawed as brought into being by the instability of the international environment.

The upset of planning targets is one obvious result. Planners have also to reckon on imperfect control over national resources. An increasingly important area in which their writ runs fitfully in the short run and hardly at all over time is that of foreign investment, both foreigners' investment at home and nationals' investment abroad. Big business is now almost necessarily international. It sees the world as its sphere of activity and meets its rivals everywhere in it. To compete effectively, it might need to concentrate some parts of its range at home, and produce others abroad. This demands strict control over the manufacturing process everywhere. Almost invariably research and development is concentrated at the parent unit, and foreign subsidiaries fed from it. Official pressures to export, to save imports, to remit foreign earnings or restrain capital outflows; global taxation considerations and the tax advantage of transmuting some forms of income into others – royalties into fees, profits into commissions and so on – and adjusting the prices of supplies sent from one subsidiary to another; the desire for political insurance; and a host of other, non-technical considerations reinforce the big firm's need to control its operations from one centre, notwithstanding the political boundaries that make international operation inevitable. 'General Motors', wrote its Chairman, 'is a single world-wide enterprise in concept, organization, structure and operation.' And that goes for most.

The ability to control in this way stems from the increasing ease and speed of communication and travel. The methods of doing so are utterly inimical to planning and control by the state. This is true of decisions about the distribution of ownership in overseas affiliates, about the siting of production and research facilities, about the international flow of capital, profits, information and personnel within the firm, about the origins of exports and imports. No means of supervision and control pre-empted by a firm is open to use by the state, and *vice versa*.

More often that not, due primarily to the feebleness of planning in the west, the conflict remains latent. Occasionally it flares up, as in Gaullist France, where American penetration of the car, computer, petroleum, chemical and electrical equipment industries has given Gaullism a solid protectionist support beneath the froth of battle against '*Franglais*'. In Germany, so solemnly wedded to *laissez-faire*, the nationalist hackles are also rising. The Bundestag has heard protests against US economic penetration from people like Dr Alexander Menne, a Director of Farbwerke Hoechst, and Chairman of the Bundestag Economic Committee, and there has been a pronounced electoral swing towards strident, anti-American nationalism embodied in Franz-Josef Strauss, Minister of

Finance in the coalition Government, and, if only momentarily, a similar swing towards the neo-Nazi National Democratic Party. Even Wilson has shown signs of shedding that running-dog look: 'While Her Majesty's Government are loyal members of NATO,' he told reporters in Rome early in the year, 'we don't believe that anything in it requires us to accept the domination of European industrial and economic life by American industrial interests.'[34]

Other resources are hardly more tractable. As is shown in Part 2, planning has come increasingly to depend on wages policy – the attempt to adjust the distribution of incomes between countries by adjusting the distribution of incomes between classes *directly, without loss of output*. As such it is flawed from the start. Apart from the crucial consideration that workers are not responsible in and towards capitalist society, and therefore only partially respondent to the social consensus on which wages policies rest, there is the practical point that high employment, growth, stability and many other elements in the causal loop mentioned in the Introduction combine to scatter widely the points of actual wages struggles and to divorce them from the traditional centres of negotiation and labour diplomacy. The emphasis in a number of key industries shifts from the union official (and employers' organization) to the workplace representative (and local management), from the centre where national considerations prevail to the periphery where local ones do, from an environment in which high employment appears to be negotiable, something for which compromises have to be made, to one in which it is a fact of life.

The consequences of this shift are profoundly affecting the labour movement and the structure of politics throughout the west. They certainly threaten the very idea of planning. Yet they derive as naturally from high employment and its connected phenomena as does planning itself.

We are back where we started, groping for the origins of high employment and stability. While these could scarcely have been sustained for any length of time without planning (the

34. *Financial Times*, 18 January 1967.

economies and their mutual relations are inherently too volatile for that), planning itself would hardly be called for in their absence. In Britain at least, where economic policy has more often than not been directed at creating rather than alleviating unemployment, the contrary view is untenable.

2. Trade and Innovation

Stability and high employment have been traced back to the vast expansion of international trade since the war. It has been remarkable enough: in the 1950s world trade grew at an average rate of about six per cent per year, rising to seven and a half per cent annually in the sixties, and nine to ten per cent in 1963–6, compared with a rate of between five and six per cent annually in the two previous periods of fastest growth this century, 1910–14 and 1921–9. Since most of the increase has been due to more intensive trading between the developed western capitalist countries – up from two fifths of the total in 1950 to about one half today, there seems to be every reason to see in trade the key to the postwar economy.

The thesis runs as follows: high employment depends ultimately on maintaining a high rate of investment which itself depends on a widely-held expectation of an increase in demand. In the heavily trading countries of the developed west, 'the most important determinant of confident expectations about the long-run rate' of increase in demand is the buoyancy of exports'.[1] Since, with high employment, there is a strong tendency to call on world supplies to satisfy a volatile consumer demand for 'luxuries' or to break temporary supply bottlenecks, or to take advantage of a very intricate industrial specialization, international trade – particularly in manufactures – tends to grow faster than output. This in turn recharges demand expectations, investments and employment.

As in any other causal loop – the 'vicious' or 'virtuous' circles of economics – there is no real indication of priority or of the direction of causality. A roseate export perspective might indeed trigger off investment and run it round in the direction

1. W. Beckerman and Associates, *The British Economy in 1975*, Cambridge University Press, 1965, p. 46.

indicated. This is certainly true of Germany's export-led booms in 1951, 1955, 1959–60 and 1964. But it might equally be – Britain is a case in point – that the autonomous change occurs in investment and that buoyancy in a country's international trade is a natural consequence. Or high employment itself might be the initial element. Equally, it might well be – and probably is – that none of them are 'autonomous', that they all rest on some other outside factor.

The picture is something like the classic boom phase of a trade cycle, with the prospect of sales, actual investment and relatively high employment mutually reinforcing each other. But there is one difference, and that a crucial one. Under *laissez-faire*, the boom generally ended in crisis and slump as the 'virtuous circle' (confidence-accumulation-employment) careered against a wall of labour shortage or some other scarcity and turned 'vicious' – became a circle of lost confidence–no accumulation–unemployment. We now seem to be insulated from this sort of collision: there has been what, in traditional terms, amounts to a labour famine in important parts of the western capitalist world for the better part of three decades; there have been down-turns in international trade without the rest of the loop being dragged into decline; there have been stops to expansion of a general kind (as in 1952 and 1958) and in individual countries (in Britain four times since the war; in the US three times; in Italy, in France, and even in Germany); and there have been declines in the quantity of officially held international reserves. And yet the boom goes on more or less. Clearly there is little point in seeking its causes within a loop common to both boom and slump.

At this point the argument falls back a step to technical innovation. Speed-up in technical change, it runs, has pumped dynamism into international trade and so set the beneficent loop turning. It has done so by offering affluent consumers the world over a stream of new or improved goods on which to exercise their 'discretionary purchasing power', and, by offering manufacturers specialist machines and materials which are often not to be had at home or only at higher cost. On this view, 'what nations sell in international trade is, to an increasing extent, the ability to innovate quickly';[2] and innovation, trade and a quick metabolism of fixed capital merge together as the sustaining force of high employment and stability.

There is no doubt that the increasing pace of technical innovation has had something of this effect. Direct evidence on the abnormally fast growth of the trade in capital goods between the major capital-goods producing countries, or the faster-than-average growth in trade in manufactures between them is backed by a host of circumstantial evidence, from legal decisions to class know-how sales as income rather than as capital gain[3] to the mushroom growth of industrial espionage and counter-espionage services.[4] Innovation is fast becoming an industry in its own right, with predictable costs, products and markets. It is a growth industry which not only absorbs an increasing proportion of an economy's resources but increases the wastage rate of fixed capital and so creates 'opportunities of further investment'.[5] As such it has a dual value.

But it cannot claim an exogenous, independent existence. It is as much part of that loop as international trade and the direction of causality remains indeterminate. If anything, high employment is more important in stimulating innovation than innovation is in creating employment. Improbably enough, one of the most 'innovatory' industries in Britain is agriculture: 'Even miserably small farmers', runs a report,

are willing to experiment with new methods, new machines and the sort of new chemicals that would stop the average factory inspector in his tracks ... And for this there are two explanations. One is the high cost and rising shortage of farm labour, which gives farmers the incentive to try anything that looks as if it might reduce labour costs and increase labour productivity.

(the other being the 'outstandingly good advisory service run

2. Shonfield, op. cit., p. 44.
3. e.g. *Inland Revenue Commissioners* v. *Rolls Royce Limited*, 1961.
4. A recent memorandum prepared for the Federation of German Industries by Dr Riester of Mercedes Benz demands prison sentences for industrial spies (*The Times*, 18 June 1966).
5. C. F. Carter and B. R. Williams, *Investment in Innovation*, Oxford University Press, 1958, p. 17.

by the Ministry of Agriculture').[6] On a more general plane, so long as labour was plentiful and cheap, as it was more or less up to the Second World War, *extensive* investment through duplicating existing techniques is clearly the easiest method of expansion; drop this condition and *intensive* investment becomes the only way. In the one case, technical innovation is so loosely related to practical need and so unsystematically rewarded that it might give the appearance of an independent factor; in the other, it is too obviously a necessary adjunct of growth for there not to be a *system* of incentives for improvers and innovators, or to take it a step farther, for invention not to be institutionalized.

This it now largely is, in industry, in private research associations, in governmental and supranational laboratories. It is measured, compared internationally and shaped in advance. And while it is true that 'under monopoly capitalism there is no necessary correlation ... between the rate of technological progress and the volume of investment outlets',[7] it is also true that the assumption of monopoly is becoming less tenable. Everything points to fiercer, more implacable competition on a world scale. It might be economic, waged now as much with the states' resources as those of business; it might be military, waged as much with business' resources as those of the states. Whatever it is, it demands an output and an economic growth that only systematic innovation can provide.

Innovation is important. It is hardly autonomous.

6. *Economist*, 19 March 1966, p. 1148.
7. Paul A. Baran and Paul M. Sweezy, op. cit., p. 97.

3. An Arms Economy

Common to the explanations suggested so far is the assumption that we should collapse into over-production and unemployment were it not for some special offsetting factor, intended – as in the case of planning – or not – as in the others. The thesis offered here shares the assumption. Where it differs is in locating outside the causal loop itself the mechanism which sets it turning.[1]

The argument for seeing a permanent threat of over-production (*not* a threat of permanent over-production) as inseparable from capitalism rests on three empirical propositions: that the relations between different capitals are by and large competitive; that an individual capital's competitive strength is more or less related to the size and scope of its operations; and that decisions affecting the size and deployment of individual capitals are taken privately by individuals and groups which form a small segment of the society which has to live with the consequences. Were it not for the first two there would be no compulsion on each capital to grow as fast as it might through 'accumulation' (that is, saving and investment) and 'concentration' (that is, merger and takeover): were it not for the third, growth would never stumble far beyond society's offtake. Together they also define the mechanism for attaining, and retaining, stability as one that augments offtake while moderating the rate of expansion that would result.

1. 'Causal loop' might be thought too much of a good thing by now. But 'vicious' and 'virtuous' circles, the established currency, are at best incongruous in a context of material progress and social decay. The manufacture and use of napalm increase the users' national income – in economese they are therefore most decidedly part of a 'virtuous' circle. But only in economese. Ordinary language takes greater care with its value judgements.

Ideally, it should do this without altering too grossly the relations between individual capitals.

Such a mechanism is to be found in a permanent arms budget. In so far as capital is taxed to sustain expenditure on arms it is deprived of resources that might otherwise go towards further investment; in so far as expenditure on arms is expenditure on a fast-wasting end-product it constitutes a net addition to the market for 'end' goods. Since one obvious result of such expenditure is high employment and, as a direct consequence of that, rates of growth amongst the highest ever, the dampening effect of such taxation is not readily apparent. But it is not absent. Were capital left alone to invest its entire pre-tax profit, the state creating demand as and when necessary, growth rates would be very much higher. Finally, since arms are a 'luxury' in the sense that they are not used, either as instruments of production or as means of subsistence, in the production of other commodities, their production has no effect on profit rates overall, as will be explained in a moment.

The addition made by arms budgets to world spending is stupendous. In 1962, well before the war in Vietnam jerked up American (and Russian) military outlays, a United Nations study concluded that something like $120 *billion* (£43,000 million) was being spent annually on military account. This was equivalent to between eight and nine per cent of the world's output of all goods and services at the time, and to at least two thirds, if not the whole of the entire national income of all backward countries. It was very near the value of the world's annual exports of all commodities. Even more breathtaking is the comparison with investments: arms expenditure corresponded to about one half of gross capital formation throughout the world.[2]

Its significance varies enormously: eighty-five per cent of the total expenditure was made by seven countries – Britain, Canada, China, France, West Germany, Russia and the United States.[3] In the countries of western capitalism military expen-

2. United Nations, *Economic and Social Consequences of Disarmament*, New York, 1962, p. 3.
3. ibid., p. 4.

diture as a proportion of gross domestic product ranged from nearly ten per cent in the US to just under three per cent in Denmark (Britain – 6·5 per cent); and as a proportion of gross domestic fixed capital formation from nearly sixty per cent in the US to twelve per cent in Norway (Britain forty-two per cent).[4] In none was it immaterial as a market or – and this is even more important – in comparison with the resources devoted to investment.

Some industries rely heavily on arms expenditure. In the United States at the end of the fifties more than nine tenths of final demand for aircraft and parts was on government, overwhelmingly military, account; as was nearly three fifths of the demand for non-ferrous metals; over half the demand for chemicals and electronic goods; over one third the demand for communication equipment and scientific instruments; and so on down a list of eighteen major industries one tenth or more of whose final demand stemmed from government procurement. In France, the list ranged from seventy-two per cent in aircraft and parts down to eleven per cent in optical and photographic equipment.[5] In Britain, a similar list would include the aircraft industry to the extent of seventy per cent of output, industrial electronics and radio communications (thirty-five per cent each), shipbuilding (twenty-three per cent) and a number of others.[6]

The impact of arms expenditure on stability and investment is no less direct. It is heavily concentrated on the capital goods industries which are responsible for the big swings in the traditional business cycle. It provides a floor to the downswings and has, in the US, been deliberately used in this way. The fact that much of this capital equipment has no alternative use and is therefore normally included in the contract price for military

4. ibid., Table 2–1, pp. 55–7. In the UN study, the figures given for Britain are generally lower than in the more detailed report made by the Economist Intelligence Unit a year later, *The Economic Effects of Disarmament*, London: EIU, 1963. The discrepancy is not material to the argument, and no attempt is made to adjust the figures here.

5. OECD, *Government and Technical Innovation*, Paris, 1966. Table 1, p. 27.

6. EIU, op. cit., pp. 49, 65, 82, *passim*.

supplies both removes the risk element from investment and provides the wherewithal to keep it at a high level.

We have seen how high employment puts a premium on technical innovation and *intensive* investment; at one remove, on research. It is here that military outlays are of overwhelming weight as a proportion of the total, accounting for fifty-two per cent of all expenditure on research and development in the US (1962–3), thirty-nine per cent in Britain (1961–2), thirty per cent in France (1961) and fifteen per cent ('partial estimate') in Germany (1964).[7] No less than 300,000 qualified scientists are engaged on research and development for military and space purposes in the OECD area, mainly in six countries (those listed plus Canada and Belgium).[8] In Britain, 10,000 were so engaged in 1959, or one fifth of the total in research and development, supported by another 30,000 or so unqualified research workers.[9]

A lot of the research is wasted. Most is tied to contracts for particular weapons or pieces of equipment; much is scrapped when an order is cancelled (only six out of the sixteen pieces of electronic and navigational equipment developed for the British TSR-2 were salvaged from its wreckage in 1966). Costs escalate more than effort since, in the words of the Committee of Public Accounts in Britain, the Government, is 'placed at a considerable disadvantage in the price negotiations, by not having the information available to the contractor about the costs of earlier production'.[10] Purposes are sometimes confounded by the natural desire of procurement officers to make a soft landing in civvy street on retirement – 1,462 retired officers, 251 of them former generals and admirals, were on the payrolls of the 720 largest military suppliers in the US in 1960. And the largest part of the research output is kept under wraps.

7. *Government and Technical Innovation*, Table p. 30. The Economist Intelligence Unit, op. cit., p. 27, gives a figure of forty-nine per cent for Britain, 1958–9 (59·2 per cent in 1955–6).

8. *Government and Technical Innovation*, p. 29.

9. EIU, op. cit., p. 32.

10. *Second Report 1966–1967*, HC 158, 5 August 1966, p. 16. The quotation is from a section entitled 'Pricing of contracts for the Buccaneer Aircraft'.

Yet the 'spin-off' has not been negligible. Military research has been crucial in developing civilian products like air navigation systems, transport aircraft, computers, drugs, diesel locomotives (from submarine diesels), reinforced glass and so on. Long production runs for military purposes have brought other products, such as solar cells and infra-red detectors, down to mass price-ranges. Military use has perfected techniques of general use, such as gas turbines, hydraulic transmission, ultrasonic welding and a host of others. More important than all, concludes the OECD report,[11] is the fact that

... the results of military and space research have had, and will continue to have, a greater influence on civilian innovation by stimulating the general rate of technological advance. For example, the requirements of military and space research, especially for guidance and control, have led to fundamental and applied research in such fields as semi-conductors, micro-circuitry, micro-modules, energy-conversion and physical metallurgy, which are bound to have an impact on civilian technology ... In addition, techniques of planning, such as operational research, Progress Evaluation Review Technique (PERT), systems engineering and value engineering – developed initially for military and space purposes – will lead to a general increase in productive efficiency, and to a more rapid identification of opportunities for innovation. And finally, the high standard of performance and reliability required of military and space systems has led to the development of techniques of measurement, testing and control which will serve to increase the quality and reliability of products and components. In the field of electronics, this is particularly important.

As for arms expenditure and international trade, the United Nations study already quoted estimated the average annual military demand by industrial countries for some internationally-traded materials in 1958 and 1959 as 8·6 per cent of total world output of crude oil, three per cent of crude rubber, 15·2 per cent of copper, 10·3 per cent of nickel, 9·6 per cent of tin, 9·4 per cent of lead and zinc, 7·5 per cent of molybdenum, 6·8 per cent of bauxite, 5·1 per cent of iron ore, 2·7 per cent of manganese and 2·3 per cent of chromite.[12]

11. *Government and Technical Innovation*, pp. 31–2.
12. loc. cit., Table 3–3, p. 65.

The defence pork-barrel is very much a giant-company concern. In the United States, despite official attempts to expand the supplies network, the largest one hundred companies consistently receive three quarters of all arms outlay. In Britain, the eighteen largest companies (10,000 or more workers each) of those that replied to the EIU's questionnaire, with seventy-one per cent of total employment in the sample, had 75·2 per cent of total employment on arms production. It is not surprising. Only the biggest firms have the technical and technological resources to cope with the sophistication and sheer volume of arms production, or the financial base to tie down resources for the time it takes. But once they can cope, growth is guaranteed. The major arms contracts are so enormous that 'even the pretence of open tendering for orders could not be seriously kept up in some of the most valuable and important government contracts'.[13] 'It is estimated,' a US Assistant Secretary of Defense told the Joint Economic Committee of Congress in 1963, 'that to establish a new production source on the Polaris missile, for example, would require up to three years and an investment of over $100 million in facilities and special tooling.'[14] And although government auditing techniques are being perfected constantly to cope with the new dependence on single supply sources, the time-and-materials, or cost-plus, basis for major contracts removes almost all traces of risk to income – and to growth. Sometimes, guarantees are so open-ended and performance so poorly-policed that contractors go berserk and create new risks for themselves, as did Ferranti with its Bloodhound missile contract in Britain, when the firm was ultimately made to disgorge no less than £4½ million of its uncovenanted profit on a £13 million contract in 1964, or Bristol Siddeley which returned £4 million out of a £16½ million contract in 1967. Normally, however, capital is more restrained and the risks to growth suitably anaesthetized.

Finally – planning. Military spending has been crucial here. Official evidence to the effect that planning in the United States

13. Shonfield, op. cit., p. 344.
14. Quoted ibid., p. 344n.

was in direct response to Russia's ballistic missile breakthrough has already been quoted;[15] as was evidence that close supervision over private industry is becoming part of any big contract; and that modern methods of auditing and control stem directly from military needs. The same might be said of that increasingly essential tool of most large-scale planning exercises – the computer. Born out of the Second World War, its most sophisticated applications are still in military spheres, whether in solving design problems, playing 'war games' or in stock and production control – reason enough for the biggest computers to be denied export permits from the United States.

These direct effects of arms spending link up with one another in a number of ways, and together seem to go on a perpetual round without need for further stimuli. Yet not all the problems are tidied away. These might not be the only set of facts that could explain stability. Any academic economists should be able to construct a model in which savings and investment are exactly matched, and demand set at the point of full employment. The techniques present no difficulty. Non-academics have been at pains, with Strachey, to point out more pragmatically that 'Defence spending could be replaced by other forms of government spending ... houses, roads, dams, power-stations, schools, etc., etc.', or the government 'could probably effect the same purpose simply by cutting down the taxes on the smaller incomes'.[16] And there is no reason in logic to doubt them.

But capitalist reality is more intractable than planners' pens and paper. For one thing too much *productive* expenditure by the state is ruled out. Seen from the individual capitalist's corner, such expenditure would be a straight invasion of his preserve by an immensely more powerful and materially resourceful competitor; as such it needs to be fought off. Seen from that of the system, it would lead to such a rapid build-up of the capital–labour (value) ratio, to use one mode of expression, or to such a low marginal productivity of capital, to use another, and to such a low average rate of profit as a conse-

15. See above, p. 30.
16. Strachey, op. cit., pp. 243, 244.

quence, that the smallest rise in real wages would precipitate bankruptcy and slump. Shorn of technicalities, too much productive expenditure on the part of the state would both upset the balance between individual capitals and accentuate the system's bias towards over-production.

Only the last requires any explanation. It was a commonplace of classical political economy, that – to put it very roughly – in the long run and despite much offsetting growing intensity of capital would force down the rate of profit in a closed economy. The argument rested on two assumptions, both realistic: all output flows back into the system as productive consumption – ideally, there are no leakages and no choice other than to allocate total output between what would now be called investment and necessary consumption; second, that in a closed system like this the allocation would swing progressively in favour of investment (increasing capital intensity or – in Marx – raising the organic composition of capital). The first assumption is the pivotal one. If dropped, and the ratio of the returns to capital and to labour becomes indeterminate, the second falls and the 'law' with it.

Marx pointed to existing leaks – capitalist personal consumption ('luxuries') and gold production – but realistically chose to ignore them. He was, after all, hewing a system from brute rock, and they were neither here nor there in practice at the time. Later non-Marxist theorists within the classical tradition, forced to refine the model and also writing in a more affluent age, probed deeper into this non-productive 'Department III'. Von Bortkiewicz showed, in a paper published in 1907, that the capital–labour (value) ratio in luxury goods production (for the personal consumption of capitalists) has no part in determining the rate of profit.[17] Sraffa, in by far the most

17. Ladislaus von Bortkiewicz, 'On the Correction of Marx's Fundamental Theoretical Construction in the Third Volume of Capital', *Jahrbücher für Nationalökonomie und Statistik*, translated and printed as an Appendix in P. M. Sweezy (ed.), Eugen von Böhm-Bawerk's *Karl Marx and the Close of his System* and Rudolf Hilferding's, *Böhm-Bawerk's Criticism of Marx*, New York: Augustus M. Kelly, 1949, and effectively summarized in P. M. Sweezy, *The Theory of Capitalist Development*, Dennis Dobson, 1949, pp. 115–25.

ambitious refinement of a 'classical' system to date, showed more generally that

'luxury' products which are not used, whether as instruments of production or as articles of subsistence, in the production of others . . . have no part in the determination of the system. Their role is purely passive. If an invention were to reduce by half the quantity of each of the means of production which are required to produce a unit of a 'luxury' commodity of this type, the commodity itself would be halved in price, but there would be no further consequences; the price-relations of the other products and the rate of profits would remain unaffected. But if such a change occurred in the production of a commodity of the opposite type, which *does* enter the means of production, all prices would be affected and the rate of profits would be changed.[18]

While Sraffa characteristically refrains from adducing examples, nothing conforms so closely to the concept of 'luxuries' as arms – which cannot under any circumstances enter the production of other commodities – and certainly nothing can begin to compare in size and significance. Seen from the angle of the system, that is of pure theory, arms production is the key, and seemingly permanent, offset to the 'tendency of the rate of profit to fall'.

But this is only one constraint on the state's freedom to adopt non-military production as a stabilizer – and the less convincing perhaps for being argued from first principles. A second, practical one, is that arms production has a 'domino effect': starting in one country, it proliferates inexorably through the system, compelling the other major economies to enter a competitive arms race, and so pulling them into the stabilizer's sphere of operations.

There seems to be no other way. While the planlessness, or competitiveness, or 'anarchy of production' within each national sphere has been tempered by government intervention, so that spontaneous decisions of individual capitals are to some extent pre-ordained by decisions covering a wider sphere, anarchy remains very nearly absolute internationally. Even for

18. Piero Sraffa, *The Production of Commodities by Means of Commodities*, Cambridge University Press, 1960, pp. 7–8.

small economies, tightly constrained though they be, there are no coercive authorities more extensive than the nation state. Internationally, the system still forms in the classic manner through constant, mutual adjustment by national capitals. This is why so homogeneous a set as the countries of mature western capitalism still need to regulate their relations by means of gold – the very essence of classic capitalist mysticism about social relations. It is why the even more homogeneous set of East European countries have been unable to do more than inch beyond bilateral trading as the characteristic expression of their mutual relations. The void between competitive reality and the illusion of collaboration within closely knit blocs is immense. Between them it is immeasurable.

In the circumstances any country opting for high employment and stability through productive investments or even unproductive 'hole-filling' public works is bound to suffer in world competition. High employment might be achieved, but it might be achieved in isolation; and the result would almost certainly be a degree of inflation that would prise the single economy out of world markets. For it to endure, the ability of others to undermine it must be contained and high employment itself exported, and what better compulsion to 'buy' it than an external military threat?

It is this logic that makes nonsense of substituting a space race for an arms race. Leaving aside peaceful fall-outs like satellite communications which are no different in economic effect to any other productive investment, advances in space technology are either of potential military value and therefore demand a matching effort as insistently as, say, military nuclear or rocket technology, or they can be ignored as being a particularly effective form of hole-filling. In practice, it is the military potential that provides the dollars or the roubles on which to hang the ballyhoo of national prestige.

None of this implies that an arms budget was ever adopted anywhere as a means of securing an international environment conducive to stability. One can admit that governments usually step up their arms bills under protest; that the major steps have not necessarily coincided with economic downturns; that, in

short, the *situation* has often been seen as unfortunate, restrictive, imposed from outside or whatever; one can admit that the
initial plunge into a permanent arms economy was random –
without affecting the issue. The important point is that the very
existence of national military machines of the current size,
however happened upon, both increases the chance of economic
stability and compels other states to adopt a definite type of
response and behaviour *which requires no policing* by some
overall authority. The sum of these responses constitutes a
system whose elements are both interdependent and independent of each other, held together by mutual compulsion – in
short, a traditional capitalist system.

Once adopted, if only by chance, an arms economy becomes
necessary. It is not merely that a system of mutual compulsion
through military threat is more imperative than any other, but
that it becomes difficult to unscramble military from economic
competition. They fuse. As appears to be happening now, with
Russia and the United States adopting the frighteningly expensive anti-ballistic missile systems (ABMs) – deployment of the
US Nike-X system in earnest could cost anywhere between
$30 and $50 billion – the arms race might be speeded up not
for any real increase in military effectiveness, but in order to
increase the cost for the competitor. As *The Times* Defence
Correspondent put it, the decision to introduce the systems now
available to both sides 'makes sense only if they mean to
declare all-out *economic war* against each other, both confident
that the basic advantages of their respective economic systems
would win in the end; both confident that the pressure of this
crippling new weapons burden would cause the other side's
economy to break first'.[19] It is even rational in the disenchanted
logic of military-economic strategy to see in peace an offensive
weapon capable of disrupting industry, and requiring therefore
the 'hot-line-cold-storage' counter-strategy of stockpiling to the
next bout of hostilities. On the other hand, the original decision
to raise the ante could equally well be a rational response on
the part of either the US or Russia to a real or imagined threat
from outside the system of major deterrence, say from China,

19. *The Times*, 10 May 1966. Emphasis added.

and the equally rational mutual suspicion that ensues regardless of cause. Although earnestly meant at the time, McNamara's assurance – following China's H-Bomb explosion of June 1967 – that 'light' ABM systems on both sides would not 'destabilize' Russian–American relations expressed hope rather than conviction. In the event it was a hope quickly snuffed.

That is between 'enemies' as it were. As for relations between 'friends', members of the western coalition have learned that common defence can be made to stretch beyond common interest and be used as a cover for the particular interests of particular industries in particular countries. Under a two-year agreement ending 30 June 1967, Germany promised to buy 5,400 million marks' worth of arms and equipment from the United States to offset American military expenditure in Germany. Ten months before the end of the period, orders for nearly one half of the total were still not placed, and no more were in sight, for, as the *Economist* pointed out, 'Germany's obligation to buy so much military equipment from America ... constitutes a grave disadvantage to German industry, particularly the aircraft industry'.[20] It also constitutes a grave disadvantage to British industry forlornly looking for a niche in the German arms market.

It is difficult to exaggerate the importance of arms production and sales as the cutting edge of international competition in general. The US's successes in engrossing the western market for sophisticated weaponry and in exploiting its predominance, in ways as different as binding the NATO alliance or preventing French sales of aircraft to South Africa, has probably done more to foster European unity than anything else. At the second-class-power level, we are told that 'Britain's special position [in the US] will last only so long as her native military technology is kept going', and warned that 'there are signs that France will soon, if she does not already, command more American respect and interest in cooperation in the field' of military nucleonics.[21] Perhaps most convincing of all is the way arms sales have been organized as an integral part of inter-

20. *Economist*, 21 May 1966, pp. 809–10.
21. *The Times*, Defence Correspondent, 9 December 1966.

and intra-bloc competition. The United States have their arms-salesman in chief, in Henry Kuss, Deputy Assistant Secretary of Defense, recipient of the Meritorious Civilian Service Medal in recognition of his bulging order books (about 5\frac{1}{2}$ billion in 1967; six hundred per cent up in ten years), and head of a staff of twenty-seven civilians who handle what are called 'international logistics negotiations'. The British Labour Government have found it possible to appoint a Minister for Disarmament *and* a Head of Defence Sales, the latter – on loan from his own fast-growing arms firm – with powers to set up special export lines, to influence design 'at the formative stages',[22] to control delivery dates, utilize the diplomatic service and so on. For, explained the Foreign Secretary, 'until we can get a widespread measure of disarmament by international agreement, it is reasonable that this country should have a reasonable share of the arms market'.[23] Germany, wedded to private enterprise in this matter has had '*Waffen-und Luftrüstungs A G*' active in newly independent countries since 1963; France is officially busy, particularly amongst the victims of international boycotts from Israel to South Africa. And so on merrily.

Not all is competition all the time. East–West relations are punctuated by agreements which have contained the worst hazards so far – spiking Cuba's missiles in 1961, a limited test-ban treaty in 1963, a Middle Eastern settlement in 1967, perhaps a non-proliferation treaty soon. It is conceivable, though unlikely, that they might contain the horrendous waste and nonsense of the ABM systems. But the agreements are best understood as attempts to bring new technical and political factors into the system of mutual compulsion rather than as an approach to collaboration around shared purposes. Amongst allies agreement is naturally more common, but hardly less unstable. Given the changing kaleidoscopes of advantage as seen from national capitals, how long will the President remain willing to waive the Buy American Act on which sales of British war material to the US depend? Or how long can the West

22. *The Times*, 12 May 1966.
23. Reported from the House of Commons, *The Times*, 24 May 1966.

European countries rely on the US's voluntary exclusion from East European markets? In the latter case at least, the sands are rapidly running out.

The assimilation of arms competition into the total economy has far-reaching consequences. The arms budget's flexibility as a stabilizer *within* each national economy is set at risk by its mediation *between* economies. To expand armaments for good national economic reasons as the US was doing in 1960–61 to offset approaching recession invites retaliatory escalation for equally good international strategic reasons. There is nothing to ensure that escalation stops at the point of stability. Even if the unlikely occurs and it does stop there for one country, it would require a heroic coincidence for that to be a point of stability for others, if only because of the different sizes, structures, stages of development, sets of alliances and suchlike of the national economies grouped around a shared military technology. So that at any one time, some would be favouring a reduction in armaments to safeguard their civilian competitive position, others standing pat and others pushing for further expenditure. The current disarray of NATO, with France withdrawn, the US, Britain and Germany squabbling over support costs and nuclear sharing, the US straining to jack up European arms expenditure and Europe resisting, hardly requires a different explanation. For that matter, neither does the confusion in the Warsaw Pact, where Rumania is successfully gaulling Russia. In both cases, there seems no way of harnessing strategic and economic expediency so that they pull in the same direction.

Nor can there be. In a *war* economy the limits to the outlay on arms are set by physical resources and the willingness of the population to endure slaughter and privation. In an *arms* economy, the capacity of the economy to compete overall, in destructive potential as well as in more traditional forms, adds a further major constraint, and with it a nest of complications.

One is the difficulty of gauging a 'necessary' defence effort. As it is, all but the super-powers are being squeezed out by the growing cost and complexity of the key weapons systems. Military expenditure has also taken a hard knock from the suicidal nature of much 'defence' equipment. Even apart from these, the fact that *limited* preparedness – the sort implicit in an arms economy – does not necessarily draw fire, has not yet done so, makes the setting of the limits subject to endless debate, particularly amongst the lesser members of the western coalition that are least able to stand the economic pace and most attracted to the new opportunities for trade with the Eastern bloc. The stage is set for a slow competitive erosion of arms expenditure. The facts are eloquent. Neither Cuba nor Vietnam has reversed the declining trend in western arms expenditure – as a proportion of government spending they have dropped from twenty-five per cent in 1955 to seventeen per cent in 1965, and as a proportion of gross national product, from 7·2 per cent in 1953 to four per cent (unweighted averages). This is scarcely a stable situation.

A related difficulty is the freer play for recessionary tendencies allowed by a declining ceiling on arms outlay. This can be exaggerated. Even in its classic, *laissez-faire* period, the changing ratio of consumption to an economy's investible surplus put a floor to downswings. The higher the floor, the smaller, though more frequent, the swings. That floor is raised at any level of arms outlay – and very much more than would appear from the normal index used (defence expenditure as a proportion of GNP) because at *any* level it is a substantial part of the investible surplus. For reasons given in this chapter it is also more effective than any other in sustaining the seemingly self-levitating causal loop of high employment, growth and so on with which this essay began. Yet there is no denying the danger to overall stability of a decline in relative outlay.

The existence of a ceiling on outlay is important for another reason. It provides a massive incentive to increases in productivity (measured in potential deaths per dollar) and so leads to the arms industries becoming increasingly specialist and divorced from general engineering practice. As the OECD report already quoted states :

... the direct transfer to the civilian sector of products and techniques developed for military and space purposes is very small compared with the total magnitude of military and space Research and Development. Furthermore, the technological requirements of defence and space are diverging from those of civilian industry, which means that the possibilities of such direct transfer will tend to diminish.[24]

Coupled with this specialization and partly as a consequence, go a rising capital- and technological-intensity in the arms industries. On both counts they become less able to underpin full employment even at the same level of relative expenditure. At a declining one, and given the existence of some technological spin-off to civilian productivity, which makes the need more exacting, their potency as an offset becomes increasingly questionable.

It would be wilfully masochistic to attempt to illustrate the argument with figures just now when western unemployment (except in Britain and France) is near its nadir. But the US Administration's obvious concern at the direction of change in employment in the sixties and seventies, as reflected in its evidence to the Senate Subcommittee on Employment and Manpower (1963) and in that body's Report,[25] is a fair pointer to what might happen. Another is the form unemployment takes in the here and now: rapid unplanned and unplannable technological change in the arms sector within a ceiling on expenditure, has contributed substantially to the formation of regional and industrial husks of unemployment that remain insensitive to general fiscal and monetary cures, as well as to the misery of unskilled strata unemployable by the high-flying, quick-changing technologies in use. Again, high boom and the technologically-regressive impact of the Vietnam war with its reversion to *relatively* labour-intensive products are obscuring the point, but the plight of the shipbuilding areas in Britain and in the US, the problems of the aircraft-manufacturing areas, even the problems of black Americans, owe at least something of their intensity to the changing tides of military expenditure and the increasing complexity of production for military use.

These potential sources of instability are embedded in the

24. *Government and Technical Innovation*, p. 31.
25. *Full Employment: Proposals for a Comprehensive Employment and Manpower Policy in the US*, Washington, DC, 1963.

system. If discipline is faltering in both of the Cold War camps and the claims of non-military competition seem increasingly urgent; if, partly in consequence, military technology is becoming so specialist as to lose some of its economically stabilizing features, it is ultimately because unrestrained competition between independent economies results in uneven rates of growth and hence to a constantly changing international balance of military and economic power.

As yet these elements of instability are just a smudge on the horizon. So far, the weight of the arms economy has been on the side of stability, charging and recharging the more immediate causes of high employment, and well-being. Within that stability, however, it has nurtured a set of problems as intractable as any.

Part 2. *Problems*

4. Prices

Inflation

Since the war prices have been rising almost continuously, by between two and a half and three per cent a year on average for all countries. At first, only those abnormally dependent on foreign trade, like Holland, did anything about it. Often it was welcomed as a 'safety-valve through which the pressures arising from conflicting claims have escaped without wrecking the process of cooperation . . . on which modern production depends'.[1] At worst, it was a nuisance – for stretching the pattern of income distribution in new directions and for the social dislocations that followed – but no more than that. Only towards the end of the fifties, when international integration took a sharp lurch forward did rising prices become important as a threat to the balance of payments and so to economic independence.

The immediate causes for the price rises have been different at different times. In the mid-fifties the pressure came from a sudden increase in investment; before that, at the time of the Korean War, as also in the last few years in the US, from a sharp rise in military expenditure. On other occasions it has come from a boost or even a switch in consumer spending. So different have the obvious factors been, that there is reason enough to look behind them for a more substantial explanation. And since prices have continued upwards even during a general recession – by 1·1 per cent a year on average for the European countries in 1951–4 (1·7 per cent for the US) and 2·1 per cent in 1957–8 (2·8 in the US) – the explanation needs to take in more than simple pressure of demand.

The additional factors are basically institutional. Most big firms operate with an after tax 'profit target' of between ten

1. W. B. Reddaway, 'Rising Prices for Ever?', *Lloyds Bank Review*, July 1966, p. 9.

and fifteen per cent on capital employed. Most of them hit it most of the time by adding a fixed mark-up to costs, usually 'standard' or notional unit costs at three quarters or four fifths of capacity production; or by setting a feasible selling price and designing the product to order. Whichever way it is done, if costs – real or notional – rise, this method of pricing sees to it that final prices rise too. Since big firms also concert their price changes one way or another price relationships at large tend to freeze fairly solid.

This is not always true. Big suppliers meet big purchasers; growing international integration multiplies the number of really competitive situations; new products need to carve out room for themselves by becoming steadily cheaper; and governments do fix prices, so that even the biggest firms are sometimes made to absorb higher costs. But none of this happens so often as to upset the broad conclusion that firms normally can and do pass them on to the final consumer.

One result is that an increase in taxes on business designed to dampen down inflation is almost bound to have the opposite effect – profits remain stable, the tax is passed on and prices rise even more; the corporation merely acts as an unofficial tax collector. Even more paradoxically, deflation can turn out to have an inflationary influence – as output falls below 'standard cost' levels, unit costs rise and are passed on in the same way.

Sometimes big business appears to court higher costs. In order to attract and retain scarce labour they normally pay, or are forced to pay, at the top of the going bracket. At the same time, in order to exercise some control over labour's demands, they have taken to guaranteeing wage increases in long-term wage contracts (which now cover a third or more of the manufacturing labour force in many countries). In most cases the increases are more than compensated by a rise in productivity. Sometimes they are not, and labour costs go up. More important, where big firms have a choice between resisting a wage increase and generalizing it, the advantage usually lies with the latter. As the higher labour costs radiate to smaller, less productive firms, which simply cannot hold their prices, the big ones can either tag along and pocket higher profits, or expand their share of the market at the others' expense. In some cases the bargaining system is tailored to provide this choice – in Germany, for example. There, the terms of an agreement become obligatory throughout an industry once employers with half the industry's payroll have accepted it, or if either signatory obtains official assent to extension. In practice most agreements are 'extended'.

None of this would have anything like the importance it has were it not for the behaviour of labour. For reasons that will be taken up later, there has been a widespread shift in the location of initiative and power from its central organizations to the periphery, from trade unions to formal or informal workplace committees. Because labour, particularly skilled labour, is relatively scarce these semi-autonomous bodies have achieved a leverage which can, when used, send local earnings sharply upwards. The increase might come as a straight payment on top of centrally-bargained rates. Usually it is done more indirectly by adjusting piece rates upwards and then aligning the time rates that go with them. It sometimes comes in even more devious ways through juggling with overtime and job-descriptions and even rigging 'scientific' productivity measurements, which then become negotiable issues.

However engineered, the rise acts as a signal to others to do the same, a signal amplified by the links between workers in multiplant firms, by the complacency of managements able to pass on increases, by the mobility of the workers themselves. Even official wage policies have that effect, through the publicity they give to wage gains, their stress on equal pay for equal work, and their use of comparability as an important criterion. In a good year, local wage 'drift' on these lines, or 'wage drive' as it should be called, can increase earnings directly by twice, three or even more times centrally-negotiated increases. Often, as in Sweden during the fifties, it has been the sole source of improvement in real earnings.

Its indirect effect is probably even more significant. No trade union leadership can allow workplace representatives – in many ways its competitors – to pull too far ahead. So 'drift' almost invariably precipitates attempts at 'consolidation' through higher official wage claims. The annual periods to which most figures relate leave a lot of room for other influences. There is also no real way of discovering how far union officials are persuaded by local wage drives and how far by their own estimates of what the traffic will bear. But it is significant that in every country years of fast drift are normally followed by years of big centrally negotiated wage increases. For most countries, a similar table to the one given here for Britain can be constructed. In one – Sweden since 1966 – consolidation of drift has become a recognized item in central pay settlements.

No body of workers is likely to ignore voluntarily a wage-rise signal. Comparative earnings and status are one of the few easily recognized points in the area of wage bargaining; they are the most important practical argument for trade union organization; the most commonly used criterion for trade union effectiveness; and one of the most durable counters at the bargaining table. If anything by narrowing wage differentials high employment has increased popular sensitivity to them and lowered the flashpoint for protest when they change; at the

Britain: Wage Rates and 'Drift', October 1958 to October 1966 (percentage change on previous year)

	Average hourly wage rates	'Wage Drift'
1958	+3·7	−0·6
1959	+1·3	+1·4
1960	+5·5	+2·1
1961	+6·4	+0·5
1962	+4·2	+0·2
1963	+2·3	+1·3
1964	+5·7	+2·4
1965	+7·3	+2·2
1966	+5·6	+0·9

HM Treasury, *Economic Reports* (supplements to *Economic Trends*)

same time the widening scope and growing formalization of bargaining has made comparison more 'scientific'.

Although it would be hard to find a strike that was intended purely to keep up with the Joneses or to preserve the striker's status as a Jones – such as a strike to reduce other workers' wages – it would be equally hard to find a strike that does not use some form of comparison as a major argument to management and as the binding element between the strikers themselves. It would be even harder to show a successful attempt at improving the relative position of low-paid workers as a whole. So far every national campaign to do so, the so-called 'solidaristic' campaigns to which most central trade union federations are committed, has been frustrated by the spontaneous spread of the increases negotiated to all wage brackets and the reinstatement of the original differentials.

One important consequence which derives as much from other, technological factors like quasi-automation as from the growing ease of comparison is that ever-smaller bodies of workers are able to wield ever-larger influence as wage pacemakers. In France, workers at Renault acted as the leading link in wage and holiday boosts early this decade. In Britain too it has been car workers that have made much of the running. In Germany, the metal workers act in this way; in Holland, shipbuilding and engineering workers; and in many countries, Sweden is notable here, the export sector as a whole has led the drive. Everywhere the leaders can be further identified in individual firms, plants or even sections. By pushing earnings to the limits of productivity increases in the most dynamic sectors or firms they provide a standard of comparison which, when acted upon, can push average earnings well beyond productivity increases in the economy as a whole.

Economists have called the mechanism a 'wage-wage spiral'. As the 'convention of comparison' it has become a prime target of wage-planners, earning more fire from the British Prices and Incomes Board, for example, than any other. Industrial relations experts have cast about – vainly – for 'forms of wage drift ... [that] do not spread from one group of workers to others'.[2] Managements have found it necessary to shift local wage- and rate-fixing higher and higher in the hierarchy in order to take account of it. And since circumstances are turned into hard cash and softer conditions by industrial action, and since such action is increasingly organized by workplace representatives, the battle against drift has come to mean the attempt to curtail their power. This will be taken up in Chapter 7.

Another consequence of the shift downwards in labour's bargaining power is that earnings become insulated to some degree from the general state of the labour market. So much depends on the interplay of workplace drive and managerial drift in particular circumstances, and so much on particular conditions in the sub- and sub-sub-markets for specific skills, that it could hardly be otherwise. As it is, in the US, relatively high unemployment in today's terms has not prevented rapid, almost uninterrupted advances in average earnings throughout the post-war period. In Britain, earnings have been, if anything, more autonomous.[3] The same has been reported a number of times of the European countries.[4] Individual industries have shown a similar pattern, with contraction, sackings and rising wages appearing together, as in the early fifties in British cotton textiles, or in US bituminous coal-mining throughout most of the post-war period. Within limits the press of wages goes on, insensitive to minor changes in the general labour market, and with it the press of prices.

Neither would matter much in a closed economy unless one happened to be amongst the many who cannot fight effectively for higher incomes to offset the higher prices. But in the increasingly open and integrated economies of the west prices and wage rises have become a major headache, as is shown in the

2. H. A. Turner and H. Zoetewij, *Prices, Wages and Incomes Policies in Industrialized Market Economies*, International Labour Office, 1966, pp. 133–4.

3. See for example J. C. R. Dow, op. cit., Table B. 2, p. 347.

4. See, for example, OEEC Secretariat papers on 'Wage Determination in Selected Countries', Appendix 4 in Fellner *et al.*, *The Problem of Rising Prices*, Paris, OEEC, 1961; *Wages and Labour Mobility*, Paris, OECD, 1965.

next section, and one which neither business nor labour in their present form can hope to cure directly.

Integration

Living standards in Western Europe are now roughly comparable. Industry is rapidly becoming equally important to most countries. Increasingly Carnaby Street styles the clothes, Turin the cars and the Harvard Business School the management. And hordes of tourists – seventy-five million in West Europe alone in 1965 and increasing by twelve per cent a year – are landing and leaving, comparing and adjusting.

This is not just a matter of growing similarity, but of growing mutual interdependence. At its most impressionistic, we now take it for granted that (British) Wage Increases Shock the Germans, in the words of a recent *Times* headline, or that interest rates throughout Europe shoot upwards when a US President asks businessmen to pare their investment plans abroad, or that the acreage sown to tomatoes in Sicily is determined in Brussels. Beyond the impressions there are real facts: for example, the growing integration of the six Common Market countries, whose inter-trade went up from a third to a half between 1958 and 1965 (unweighted average); or three quarters of whose agriculture is now thoroughly internationalized; and a large proportion of whose national incomes is already directly affected by the Market – ranging from eleven to twelve per cent in Germany or France to double that in the Benelux countries. And behind the Six there are even larger developments at work, decompressing the economic space between all the western capitalist countries, so that now they take from one another about half world exports where fifteen years ago they took about two fifths of a very much smaller total, or three quarters of private international capital flows, compared with well under one half. And if the success (May 1969) of the Kennedy round of tariff negotiations is anything to go on, these comparatively rich countries are prepared for even greater integration in the future.

The reasons for their growing mutual involvement are easy

to list. On a very general plane, as production gets more technologically intensive each country becomes increasingly dependent on the general stock of knowledge. How dependent, nobody can say. But if we take the major movements of scientists and know-how payments, we might get an inkling. Between 1949 and 1966, the US alone absorbed about 100,000 foreign, mostly European-trained engineers, scientists and physicians. By the end of the period they were coming in at a rate equal to one ninth of all US first degrees in engineering and nearly a third of all medical doctorates. As against this, in the two-way flow of payments for licensing, royalties, patents and so on – the 'technological balance of payments' – the US was running an annual surplus against western Europe of about a billion dollars. Not all the movement is between Europe and the US, although the bulk is, and the flow of royalty payments and scientists is only a rough indication of dependence on the stock of common knowledge, but there is enough in it to conclude that 'a large part' of the increase in productive capacity in any country 'depends ... upon innovations and technological and social progress in others'.[5]

Size is another reason for the growing mutual dependence internationally. The feasible scale of production and marketing is now such that many firms simply outgrow their national market, particularly when it has to be shared with others. Once exporting becomes necessary an international marketing organization also becomes necessary, and when this occurs, international operation – manufacturing, servicing or whatever – is only one step away. The multinational firm is born.

It has happened everywhere since the war, but nowhere with such *éclat* as in the US. Stimulated by its war-time growth, US big business crashed heavily into the rest of western capitalism during the fifties and sixties; up to 1964 their investments in Western Europe multiplied sevenfold to $12 billion, in Canada fourfold to $14 billion, mostly in manufacturing. As much as a quarter of all US industrial investment is now spent on plant and equipment outside the US, overwhelmingly in those two

5. Kuznets, op. cit., p. 17.

areas. Two fifths of all the investment that takes place in Canada is now American, and although the figure is only about six per cent for Europe overall, a substantial proportion of the stake in some very crucial industries is US-controlled. In Britain, this applies to half the market for cars and two fifths of the market for computers, oil products, tractors and agricultural machinery; in France, to around two fifths of the market for electronic machinery, tractors and agricultural machinery, and a fifth for petroleum, food and cars; in Germany, to nine tenths in petroleum, some two fifths in food, drink and tobacco and a quarter in cars and electronics. In most countries a finer breakdown would show even higher proportions in the fastest-growing branches of the chemical, pharmaceutical, electronic equipment and other research-based industries.

Since only the largest firms in an industry have the organization and resources to undertake international investment, their intrusion acts as a further stimulus to integration. At first national firms huddle together in an attempt to meet size with size, as witness the tide of amalgamations within each country mentioned in Chapter 1. Governments become active business-marriage brokers, cajoling and ultimately forcing the most reluctant partners to the altar, as has happened again and again throughout Europe, particularly in France during the current Five-Year Plan (1966–70). Some government departments in Britain have even been actively advising trade associations how to circumvent the Restrictive Trade Practices Act 'in the public interest'.

But there are limits to what can be accomplished in this way. Even where home markets can contain the scale on which most industries operate, the multinational firm can contest that market with a battery of resources that will dwarf almost anything offered by even the largest purely national firm outside the United States. They are simply out-classed. Volkswagenwerke, for example, Germany's largest enterprise, and itself more than a national firm, has an annual *turnover* hardly more than General Motors' *net profit*. Péchiney, forced against its will late in 1966 to become one of the six top French companies, one of the thirty top non-American firms and supplier of nine tenths of the aluminium used in France, has an output smaller than any of the big US aluminium fabricators, two of whom have recently moved into its home pitch. The combined British, German and French market for electronic capital goods is one fifth the size of the American, and shared by three lots of firms. The combined turnover of the twenty largest US corporations is about equal to West Germany's gross national product, the largest in Europe. And since a handful of US firms account for most of the total US stake in Europe, and they are backed by a national research expenditure twice or three times the intensity of any in Europe, the odds against purely national firms anywhere outside the US are pretty long, however well-propped-up by their governments they might be.

A private 'Federation à la carte' has gone a little way to shorten the odds, by merging know-how and resources across frontiers. There have been multinational bond issues to tap the separate national capital markets simultaneously; there has been a phenomenal growth in the Euro-dollar market, the nearest there is to a truly international one. But private federalism is often perverse. Left to itself, a European firm short on know-how or capital is more likely to line up, or submit to, a US firm, as Machines Bull have done in France or Olivetti in Italy, or Rootes in Britain, than to seek strength from another European firm similarly short on know-how and capital. There are exceptions, some of them quite important, like the Agfa-Gevaert line-up, or the looming ICI-Ilford-Ciba one, against Kodak. But they are exceptions and, if developments in the crucial science-based industries like computers and other electronic capital goods, communications, trunk-line air transport and so on are anything to go by, they have not been on anything like the scale needed to right the asymmetry of business power. Nationalism and industrial efficiency are simply diverging.

This is where public federalism comes in. The Common Market, Britain's frustrated bids to enter it, the British offer of a European Technological Community (as well as the prompt and prophylactic offer of American aid to strengthen Europe's technology) would hardly make sense but for the threat from big US business (and – although this is outside our scope – from Russia). Nor would many of the detailed initiatives of the European governments: fully half of the 1965 Memorandum to the Six on the *Establishment of European Companies* is devoted to the 'Creation of large companies'; they have made moves towards a single European capital market without which the industrial giants envisaged would wilt, and are considering measures on these lines.[6] Despite their pernicketiness about national sovereignty, some of them have been brought to cooperate in a few particularly expensive and militarily important ventures in aero-space and nuclear research. Others have mounted an effective combined operation to block the advantage that dollar companies (and to some extent sterling companies) derive from the ruling international financial arrangements.

Not even the most nationalist of national capitals could do these things alone. They have not the resources for positive steps, and negative ones, like banning US companies unilaterally, are worse than useless; either the banned stay away and the asymmetry of business power grows, or they find their way in again as they have done or threatened to do more than once in France through German, Italian or Belgian back doors. Like it or not, effective defence is integrated defence; and although the profile of integration can never be finally fixed since it follows the shape of the challenge, the distribution of business power in western capitalism ensures that the brightest spotlight falls on the integration of the rest as against the US. Even de Gaulle conceded this in practice when he reluctantly lifted the bans on US investment in France and equally reluctantly pressed further into the EEC, for as he said at the end of a visit to Bonn, July 1967, 'it is essential that the French and Germans stick together. Otherwise it will be impossible to stand up to the hegemony of America'.

6. See EEC, *The Development of a European Capital Market*, Report of a Group of Experts appointed by the EEC Commission, Brussels, 1966 (the *Segré Report*); OECD, *Capital Markets Study* (4 volumes), Paris, 1967 and 1968.

On a different plane, it is clear that fully employed economies cannot easily or quickly break bottlenecks in supply from internal production and that the availability of imports from like-structured economies is now a substitute for the flexibility that once came from having unused capacity and unemployed labour. In time, such imports develop into systematic exchanges and a more intricate international division of labour. In the fifties, to take a well-thumbed example, the developed west absorbed more than half the total increase in world imports of capital goods compared with about a quarter for the period 1899–1937. Most of the increase went to the big four producers – the US, Germany, Britain and France.

These and many other mutual dependencies – the list is hardly exhausted – are fixed in a criss-cross of institutional arrangements and formal pacts which, although not confined to the western capitalist countries, mesh thickest about them. They range from the unilateral, like the movement of European countries towards currency convertibility in the late fifties, to the multilateral like the Convention for the Settlement of Disputes Between States and the Nationals of Other States; from limited technical links like the International Air Transport Association to all-embracing bodies like the Organization for Economic Cooperation and Development; from the financial to the military; from arrangements exclusive to these countries to wholly catholic ones. They form a powerful network in their own right.

One of the most significant at present is the system of fixed exchange rates between different national currencies. Born immediately after the Second World War out of a desire to avoid the financial chaos of the thirties, and disturbed only rarely and under extreme pressure, it is now protected by a powerful coalition of interests. These range from big business, afraid of the uncertainties floating exchanges would bring to their international operations, to central bankers for whom the defence of parity has become a key weapon in asserting their independence of governments, and to the governments themselves who fear that any advantages from devaluation would be outweighed by its inflationary effects under conditions of high employment and, in some cases, by the consequences of speculation. The fixed parities system is policed by the little-known Working Party III of the OECD, made up of central bankers and top economics officials, who meet in Paris nearly every month to carry out 'multilateral surveillance' of national economic policies. By facilitating international economic flows, fixed parity promotes all the integrative forces that have been mentioned, and is immensely strengthened in the process. One example – admittedly a strong one – will show how: the Six have finally decided to institute common farm prices based on a European unit of account. In practice, this quarantines so large a part of production from the effects of currency changes that barring a really shattering international crisis these lose a lot of their credibility as policy instruments. As a result, Common Market exchange rates are very nearly fixed and the EEC itself an embryo monetary union.

Interdependence is a strenuous form of coexistence. The freer the flow of trade, capital, techniques and people, and the more mobile, the more vulnerable are the economies to mutual exposure and – as a direct result – the more are their economic policies governed by international payments considerations. In Britain, the worst hit in this way, balance-of-payments strains triggered off general deflationary measures in 1947, 1949, 1951, 1955, 1956–7, 1961, 1964, 1966, 1967 and 1968.[7] They in turn carry most of the blame for her miserable growth record. In other countries, equally drastic steps have been taken for similar reasons at one time or another since the war. In all of them, as is shown in Chapter 1, the threat of imported instability has been a prime argument for national planning. It has also been at least as strong an argument for international coordination. For as national planning widens the scope for discretion, and so for arbitrariness in economic events, it becomes increasingly important for other countries to control such planning, or at least to influence it. But so rigid are international arrangements and so anguished the process of adapting them by unanimous consent – there is no other way in a world of national sovereignties – that to orchestrate

7. And 1969.

national plans is very nearly impossible. What is left is a confused process of mutual blackmail, of forming and reforming alliances, of partial and unilateral conformity to what seems like the going pattern, and of competitive growth. It can hardly be called international planning, but it is the only form that will contain both sovereign nation states and their mutual dependence.

Direction

Separately, neither rising prices nor international integration would present the problems they do. Together, however, they form an explosive mixture. And since both are embedded deep in the structure of western capitalism – in the violent growth of the giant firm and of the economy as a whole, in high employment and the confidence that these will go on, and in much else that has been reviewed – something needs to be done to control the explosion.

This something now needs to be specific. Before the First World War it was enough for a country to wait on the automatic workings of the gold standard on employment, prices and international trade in order to retain international equilibrium. Such, at least, was the view from the bridge in Britain. Between the wars, equilibrium was achieved less automatically through devaluations, deflations, wage cuts and forced closures. But now these general price signals are so baffled by the institutional rigidities touched on here, that as often as not they fail to get through. To be effective, the monetary authorities would need to make them very strong and very punitive indeed.

At least this is how it has been in Britain. The foreign exchange cost of achieving equilibrium indirectly in this way rose from \$1,300 million in 1956 to \$7,000 million odd in 1967.[8] The human cost has gone up almost as fast: unemployment reached 2·1 per cent in the 1958 trough, 3·1 per cent – even discounting the effect of an exceptionally cold spell – in the winter of 1963. At the time of writing, it looks as if it will

8. See above, p. 39.

be more than that before the effects of the current freeze wear off. The resulting cost in growth foregone and in international competitiveness has been incalculable: Britain remains the slowest-moving country of western capitalism, and the one whose share of world exports is dropping fastest.

There is more than cost here. Indirect economic management within an acceptable range can also simply not work. Deflation – it has been shown – might have a perverse effect on prices, sending them up not down. It almost certainly has a perverse effect on labour, making it more rigid, less efficient, more costly as workers try to beat insecurity by rejecting innovation, stretching job-times or reinforcing demarcation frontiers.

More fundamentally, indirect management is powerless to affect workers' motivations. Capital has always sought – and nearly always obtained – a strictly defined level of performance from labour, and has always tried to impose a clear code of workshop behaviour. In exchange, workers have traditionally been free to live apart – in slums maybe, but also in a socially and mentally distinct world, the 'state within a state' so proudly advertised by Social Democracy before the war, and whose remains are still liberally scattered in the European labour movements. In a sense they were compelled to create this world or have their humanity destroyed by the normless violence of early capitalism. But, just as important, they were left more or less free to do so.

This is no longer the case. As production becomes more complex and the cost of physical plant per worker grows, workers' education, skills and concentration grow in importance; and the use they make of their free time of increasing concern. Given the skilled nature of so many jobs and the difficulties in setting formal work-patterns – partially reflected in the swing-back from piece-rates to time-rates and to hybrid piece-time systems – their discretionary behaviour at work becomes more important and the degree to which they are involved in production-goals crucial.

One measure of the change is the mushrooming of industrial psychology and sociology in the universities, or of personnel departments in big firms. Another, related change, is the wide-spread and growing impatience with a purely behaviourist approach to labour discipline as implied in deflation and its like, and the equally widespread adoption of wages and labour policies to affect positively and directly labour's independent decisions. The point is not that deflation or general regulation are out and direct state control or discrimination in – writing in the eye of Britain's worst deflationary storm since the war, this needs no stressing – but that deflation is subtly but steadily being demoted from its position as supreme adjuster to being one of a number of possible techniques, used in conjunction with others, compared with them on effectiveness and cost. As often as not, it is only part of a larger package designed less to effect a once-for-all change than to shift the weight from indirect to direct methods of control, above all, from deflation itself to wages policy.

The current bout in Britain is a case in point. At least in stated intention, 'the measures that have been taken ... are not negative exercises in the old routine: they will be used to produce a springboard for further expansion' once two conditions – 'increasing productivity' and 'the prices and incomes policy' – are accepted in practice. Thus Wilson at the Trades Union Congress, September 1966. And thus, in different tones and accents, most European governments at one time or another since the war: deflation is not *per se*, but to reveal the stops for a different economic tune. In France, whatever approaches have been made towards wages policies – in 1958 and 1962–3 – have been as part of deflationary 'stabilization plans'; in Belgium, the first serious attempt at wages planning came in 1960 as part of a projected two-year wages-stop; in Denmark, wages policies and 'stabilization' were harnessed together in 1963; in Italy, the first proposals for a wages policy came with the 'anti-conjunctural' measures, or straight deflation, of 1963.

The shift towards a direct approach, towards control rather than management, is not confined to labour. Instructions to banks on loan ceilings, to firms on investments, to hire-purchase companies on credit terms are becoming more frequent. Monopoly legislation – toothless though it still is – has spread widely through the system; control over prices is not unknown. But increasingly the beat has fallen on labour. Direction, planning itself, depends as never before on its positive control.

5. Wages

Policies

In the last few years there has been a widespread shift in emphasis from planning in general to 'forward and active manpower policies'. It would be wrong to see in this the untroubled, immanent working out of class bias in terms of economic policy. Each step could be justified by the inadequacies of the previous one. In many countries the final transition was forced by a particularly determined wage offensive: important strikes of electricians and engineering workers in Italy, winter 1962–3; a metal workers' strike in Baden-Württemburg, Germany, spring 1963; a miners' strike in France, late 1963. In others it came after labour refused to take the strain off the balance of payments, as in Britain during each of the four post-war wage stops, or in the US in 1962, or France in the late fifties and early sixties. But it would be as wrong to ignore the asymmetry of class power. Once events forced some sort of a planning structure into being, labour rather than capital was cast as the strainbearing member.

This explains how wage-restraint, or 'incomes' policies came to be pursued with special zeal in relatively low-wage countries. For example, in Holland, pioneer in the field, where industrial labour costs have been amongst the lowest in Europe since the war, three quarters the levels ruling in Britain, France, or Germany, even lower than Italy's, as late as 1959. In Britain too, most recent and important convert to official wages policies, labour costs at the operative time (early sixties) were low on the European scale: consistently lower than in Germany and France in chemicals, shipbuilding, vehicles, steel and electrical engineering; lower than any of the Common Market countries in steel; and only marginally above Italy in most.[1]

1. See G. L. Reid, 'Supplementary Labour Costs in Europe and Britain', in G. L. Reid and D. J. Robertson (eds.), op. cit., Table 33, p. 119.

But none of that matters. The important fact is that both Britain and Holland are peculiarly vulnerable to external economic forces; in both, capital is relatively concentrated and has found it fairly easy to shrug most of the burden of adjustment directly on to labour.

The asymmetry of power explains the further paradox – that wages policies are adopted despite the flimsiest of theoretical foundations. The key concept – productivity – can relate to gross or net output, to output including military production or excluding it, to total output or the output of an industry or even of a single plant. It can be measured in terms of 'weighted' or 'unweighted' man-hours, that is, in terms of simple undifferentiated labour or of labour somehow enriched – and this presents mind-cracking difficulties – with quality and skill. The difference on the last score alone can be substantial. Depending on the definition used, US output rose by either 1·6 per cent per year on average between 1889 and 1953 or 2·2 per cent, nearly half as much again.[2]

Assuming we arrive at a definition, operating the rules can be daunting. Are wages to be cut when productivity falls? Or raised when it rises even if other conditions – say, the external balance – indicate restraint? A productivity criterion, such as recommended by the Brussels Commission 'might well', *The Times* European Economic Correspondent pointed out on one occasion, 'give Italian unions strong grounds for harder bargaining'.[3] Italian unions are hardly unique. Besides, who is responsible for productivity – management or workers? And where management is clearly at fault, are some workers to forego rises accruing to others elsewhere?

The difficulties are inexhaustible and, since they stem ultimately from disputes about the position of the worker in society and the nature of work itself, they are insoluble without deeper change. They have led students of the problem to conclude

2. Turner and Zoetewij, op. cit., p. 117.
3. *The Times*, 19 July 1966.

that 'constant and perfect control' is an 'impossible task'[4] and to warn that 'it seems inadvisable to expect too much consistency from national wage policy'.[5] But policy makers are in no position to resile in the same way. They have to act, and do so in the only way open to them – through regulation and legislation. That the result – in all but straight wage freezes – normally turns into a tangle of scholastic complexity is hardly surprising.

Take Holland. Guiding principles adopted in the summer of 1959 took into account increases in productivity attained and expected in individual firms, zoning differentials, profit-sharing arrangements, pensions and savings schemes, levels of employment in different sectors, the likely effect of wages and of prices on the general level of wage differentials between firms and sectors, the length of wage contracts, and the length of the working week. It was, you might say, complex. A 'clarification' was issued in October. It specified the base periods for productivity measurements for contracts of different dates; the divergencies permitted between actual and indicated wages and their permitted time limits; the different forms of payments of increases during contracts of different duration; and the methods of calculating them. Within a year new difficulties arose 'as to what other criteria, such as profits or earning power, it would be desirable to take into account together with labour productivity in determining the permissible rate of wage advance in each industry'.[6] By 1962 the system had become so involved that the government produced a new formula: 'Take the average annual productivity increase over a previous period. Multiply this by three. Add two. Divide by four. Results = the wage increase permitted.'[7] This too was found unworkable, a flood of wage claims inundated the country the following year and wages policy other than is implied in deflation was

4. John Corina, 'Labour and Incomes Policy', *New Society*, 19 November 1964, p. 8.

5. Turner and Zoetewij, op. cit., p. 134.

6. OEEC Secretariat, 'Wage Determination in the Netherlands', in Fellner *et al.*, op. cit., p. 386.

7. Jossleyn Hennessy, 'Incomes Policies in Europe', *New Society*, 19 March 1964, p. 15.

abandoned in practice well before its formal abolition in December 1967.

Like so much else, modern labour planning can be traced back to the wars, particularly the Second World War. The key problem – to get maximum production from a fully-stretched labour force with minimum loss to higher consumption – is the same. And, allowing for the difference between a war economy and an unstable arms economy, many of the solutions adopted bear a family resemblance. They include an elaborate legal framework designed amongst other things to limit collective bargaining; a complex system of joint consultation, conciliation and arbitration; statutory wage and price control; a massive output of propaganda and 'stimuli' ranging in the disenchanted reckoning of one writer of the time, 'from appeals to duty and patriotism and calls for the defence of democracy and freedom to Aid for Russia appeals; from creating hopes or fears to establishing a self-interest or imposing penalties; from promises of a better world in the future to present improvements in social and material conditions'.[8]

The first attempts at wages planning in peace time came immediately after the war. However, it was not until the late fifties after the liberalization of western trade and payments that they became at all widespread and systematic. Until 1957 the only country with a fully-fledged and continuing wages policy – and an official apparatus to implement it – was the Netherlands. Then Austria set up a joint Wage and Price Commission through which the government associated itself with the existing tightly centralized wage-bargaining system; and in Britain the (Cohen) Council on Prices, Productivity and Incomes was appointed 'to keep under review changes in prices, productivity and the level of incomes . . . and to report thereon from time to time'. In the sixties attempts at state control really got under way: in 1961 the Austrian Commission increased its powers to formulate general principles of wage and price

8. F. A. Burchardt, 'Output and Employment Policy', *Bulletin of the Institute of Statistics*, Oxford, 31 January 1942, reprinted in University of Oxford Institute of Statistics, *Studies in War Economics*, Basil Blackwell, 1947, pp. 29–30.

adjustment. In 1962, the US stepped gingerly into the 'Cohen Council' stage with a 'guide-post' for wage adjustments and the first of a series of annual White House economic conferences to discuss wage and price levels; in Britain the short-lived National Incomes Commission was set up; and in Denmark, a somewhat toughened 'Cohen Council', the Economic Council, was constituted, its first report providing the basis for the comprehensive programme of price and wage stabilization inaugurated the following year. That year – 1963 – was a vintage one for wages-policy initiatives: Germany erected 'guide lines' for wage increases and set up its Council of Experts to review and advise; the Netherlands' Social and Economic Council was refurbished with formal powers; the Austrian Commission was strengthened; and even in France, where the Communist Party-led Confédération Générale du Travail (CGT) had long blocked real progress towards wages planning outside the state sector, an Incomes Conference (October 1963 – January 1964) agreed to try out a rudimentary system of wage-targeting and monitoring. Since then Britain under Labour has made most of the running, with the *Statement of Intent on Productivity, Prices and Incomes* signed by trade unions and business organizations in December 1964, the Prices and Incomes Board to monitor wage (and price) increases and the full-blown 'Prices and Incomes Standstill' of 1966–7.

Meanwhile in countries with centralized wage bargaining ostensibly independent of government control, official views have prevailed increasingly in practice. This has happened in all the Scandinavian countries, particularly in Norway where government intervention has been decisive in most wage settlements since the mid-fifties. And in countries that for one reason or another have fought shy of both formal wage planning and central bargaining implicit wage policies have become increasingly noticeable, as in France in 1958 when a wages policy was announced 'consistent with, and an integral part of stabilization aims',[9] or Belgium in 1960, and twice again in France in connexion with subsequent stabilization programmes.

9. Fellner *et al.*, op. cit., p. 62.

Pressures

Most trade unions have not agreed to wages policies. Overt
and effective opposition has come from the largest trade union
federations in France (CGT) and in Italy (the Confederazione
Generale Italiano del Lavoro, CGIL). Similar opposition
quashed moves in that direction in Belgium in the early sixties.
In the US, the Administration's guide-posts have been repeatedly hacked down – most dramatically during a six-week official
strike of airline machinists in mid-1966. In Britain, although
the unions did accept wages planning when a Labour Government was returned (1964) and it looked as though such planning
might be fixed into a larger context, acceptance was far from
unanimous or wholehearted. Outright opposition came from
leaders of a number of small, fast-growing technicians' unions
(draughtsmen, supervisors, scientific workers, camera crews
and technical civil servants) or small skilled groups in declining
industries (boilermakers); conditional opposition came from
some of the numerically mightiest in the land including the
mightiest – the Transport and General Workers' Union; and
many that agreed to a wages policy initially – among them
seamen, bakers, firemen, town hall officers – withdrew
their consent at the crunch. Even in the small countries
in which trade-union leaders have long accepted responsibility
for official wages policies – Holland, Austria and, with reservations, the Scandinavian countries – bouts of restiveness
and, occasionally, opposition, have punctuated their long-term
docility.

The reasons are substantial. Trade union penetration of the
labour force is everywhere fairly modest – around forty per
cent in Britain, sixteen in France, twenty-two in the US, forty-
five in Sweden – and their pull on the unorganized weak enough
without the disadvantage of having to restrict their demands.
'We shall have extreme difficulty,' the Draughtsmen's General
Secretary warned the TUC in Britain, 'in persuading technicians in the present circumstances to accept the need to pay
trade union subscriptions, in return for which their wages will
be frozen.' Besides, those already in the unions are not bonded
in: if they 'failed to convince their members that as a result

of the unions their standard of living was better, they would reject the unions'.[10]

Even where commitment to trade unionism is high, commitment to a particular union is often not, so that members find it possible to shop around. 'Hull dockers', went one report, 'received a leaflet in which one union backed the freeze while the other refused. Is it unreasonable to assume that T and GWU cards will soon be at a premium, while NUGMW cards will be ten a penny?'[11] While 'no poaching' agreements, amalgamations and closer policy coordination between unions can do something to mitigate the problem, they cannot do much. Except in Germany, there are so many competing organizations – six hundred odd in Britain, nearly two hundred in the US, 150 in France, almost ninety in Holland, 75 in Sweden, and so on – and each has so much to gain from a singleminded concentration on growth, that in the end the most binding agreements dissolve. White-collar unions and those penetrating new skill-intensive industries are particularly aggressive here: theirs are the growth occupations; their penetration ratios are mostly very low; they are the most exposed to workers and attitudes which demand tangible results from organization; they also have the least to lose from upsetting the entrenched powers of the trade union world – in Britain white-collar unions broadly defined accounted for two million out of the nine million affiliated to the TUC in 1966, but only for six out of thirty-six seats on its General Council.

Most inhibiting of all to the union leaderships is the challenge presented by the workplace organizations which, as is shown in Chapter 7, are everywhere increasing their scope and power. 'Factory organizations,' warned the General Secretary of another small, fast-growing white-collar union in Britain when explaining his opposition to wages policies, 'will turn drift into riptide. There will be a transfer of power from those who formally hold it to those informally willing to exer-

10. George Doughty, General Secretary, Draughtsmen's and Allied Technicians' Association, as reported in *The Times*, 8 September 1966.
11. *The Week*, 24 August 1966, p. 1.

cise it.'[12] Nothing is more terrible for a trade-union leader than the cry at the grass roots – 'We are the union!'[13]

The rank and file's self-assertion is a nuisance and a threat to the union leadership. But it also represents a powerful tradition, and as such is bound to strike a chord of sympathy. If the function of the leadership is to get 'more', until recently they carried it out without much thought for the larger consequences of what they were doing. Unions were not very big; the labour market was more imperfect than it is, so that gains were slow to spread from one area to another or from one trade to the next; and the economy as a whole was too loosely geared internationally to be penalized for such as did spread. Trade-union leaders could afford to be exclusively responsible to their members and so seemingly irresponsible to society at large. This was always a very partial irresponsibility, more in evidence during the stormy upheavals that went into the making of each national labour movement than in the long intervals of consolidation, more apparent during periods of stability and growth than in crisis or war, and always eager to retreat when it seemed to be challenging the system as a whole. Yet it did exist, solidly enough to have sustained that separate, semi-autonomous 'world of labour' mentioned in Chapter 4; and solidly enough to provide a real bond – of defiance towards established society – between union leaders and led.

The tradition is not exhausted. The social landscape, in Europe particularly, is thick with the rundown but not discarded institutions of a segregated existence. It is a tradition strong enough to have kept the Trades Union Congress havering for nearly two years before presenting its evidence to the Royal Commission on Trade Unions and Employers' Associations; and to have prevented it even then from fully answering the anguished: 'What are we here for?' of its own General Secretary. It lingers on, adapted to conditions of high employ-

12. Clive Jenkins, General Secretary, Association of Supervisory Staffs, Executives and Technicians, *Tribune*, 30 April 1964.
13. Title of the lead article in the first issue of an unofficial printing workers' journal, Amsterdam 1963, after three years of agitation for higher wages, unofficial strikes and campaigns to democratize the union.

ment and stability, in the obstinate defence of collective bargaining put up by the established left in the trade-union leadership, whether Frank Cousins of the Transport Workers in Britain, Otto Brenner, the Metal Workers' leader in Germany, the ideological heirs of André Rénard, late General Secretary of the Fédération Générale des Travailleurs Belges, or the majority leadership of the CGIL in Italy. It is even strong enough to exert a pull on the union leaders who have taken the plunge, as the TUC showed early in 1967, when rejecting compulsory wage restraint in favour of a voluntary system, managed jointly with the Confederation of British Industry.

Yet the tradition of apartness and of irresponsibility towards established society are under immense pressure. Capitalism has been so shaken these last fifty years by war, revolution and depression, and each national entity bar the North American has been so close to extinction at one time or another that only the very blind – or the very motivated ideologically – could have escaped some sort of explicit partisanship. Besides, it hardly bears repeating, the major trade unions are now very much larger than they were, both absolutely and in proportion to the labour force; they deal with gigantic firms on a scale and in circumstances which affect the entire economy; and no national economy can now escape the backlash of international integration. Then again, where once the national economy existed first and was conceptualized later so to speak, so that there was little or no risk in a strategy of response, planning has now reversed the order. *Decisions* about economic structure, behaviour and direction are now taken; decisions that ultimately affect the functions and status of the union leaders themselves. Not to participate in them or assume responsibility for their outcome is self-defeating. Finally, come a host of supporting pressures, whether the cementing power of social ambition now that high trade union office is an avenue to government appointment and a key to personal and social security; or the persuasiveness of an ideology centred on nation rather than class; even subventions from the state. Whatever the precise mixture, there has been a powerful thrust within the unions to abandon the exclusive 'world of labour' and join 'civil society' throughout the west; and there has been a corresponding recognition on the part of that society of the unions as an interest rather than a constraint.

This has gone on everywhere. As in many things, the first break came with the First World War when Labour or Social Democratic Ministers were brought into governing coalitions on both sides of the trenches and 'a host of Labour representatives', in the words of a recent British critic, '... acquired a stake, if not in the country, at least in the country's official business'.[14] But it was not until the Second World War that the (Allied) unions' right of access to government was finally and permanently established. Since then they have become so entrenched that the currents of normal political change hardly disturb them.

The British example is fairly typical. Nervous about its new-found freedom in Whitehall, the TUC hastened to assure the first post-war Conservative Government that –

... It is our longstanding practice to seek to work amicably with whatever Government is in power and through consultation jointly with Ministers and with the other side of industry to find practical solutions to the social and economic problems facing this country. There need be no doubt, therefore, of the attitude of the TUC towards the new Government.[15]

The Conservatives reciprocated. As 'a leading trade unionist' reported in 1957, 'If I want to talk to the Minister, I just pick up that telephone.'[16] Since then the traffic of trade-union rumps towards the proliferating seats of government administration and consultancy has been heavy. Big NEDC and 'little Neddies', the Prices and Incomes Board, the regional planning bodies, the multitude of committees and advisory bodies that both Conservatives and Labour have surrounded themselves with since the war have all received their quota. The six govern-

14. Ralph Miliband, *Parliamentary Socialism*, Merlin Press edition, p. 47.
15. TUC *Report 1952*, p. 300.
16. Martin Harrison, *Trade Unions and the Labour Party Since 1945*, George Allen & Unwin, 1960, p. 295.

ment committees on which the TUC were represented in 1934–5, grew to 60 in 1949, to 81 in 1954[17] and now stands well above the 100 mark.[18]

British trade unions are not especially privileged. 'In several European countries,' write Turner and Zoetewij in a chapter devoted to the methods and institutions of wages policies:

... organized group interests now exert considerable influence on government policy through official channels (for instance, through social and economic councils) with a view to supplanting traditional parliamentary systems. Such formal and public channels of communication and pressure have been found more useful and less devious than informal and more obscure forms of lobbying.[19]

Some of the most abstentionist trade union bodies are being drawn into the charmed circle of advice and consent: in Italy, the CGIL's isolationism is beginning to wear thin (see below). Even the CGT in France, frozen for so long in a posture of formal unaccountability for the system and its works, is thawing. Speaking officially for his Confederation and while reiterating its policy of sending officials to the Commissariat du Plan 'as *observers*, not as *participants*', the Secretary of its Economic Department conceded that 'the Plan leaves some room for change, though very little, in education, health and the like, where for reasons it would be useless to repeat here, we can exert a certain pressure'.[20] As yet, however, the shift is only a gleam in a planner's eye.

Attaching the Unions

A tried method of strengthening the official trade union will is to pin down wages in the state sector. The state is by far the largest employer in any country and its domestic arrangements have wide repercussions. In Britain, health workers and busmen

17. V. L. Allen, *Trade Unions and the Government*, Longmans, 1960, pp. 32, 34.
18. See *ABC of the TUC*, 1966, pp. 10, 11, 23–4, for an incomplete listing of 115 items.
19. Turner and Zoetewij, op. cit., p. 103.
20. *International Socialist Journal*, December 1966, p. 571.

bore the brunt of the 1957–8 wage plateau; teachers and civil servants were caught out by the 1961 pay pause; railway workers were among the first victims of the 1964 restraint. In France, where 'in contrast to previous stabilization efforts' wage pegging was successful in 1958, it was 'noteworthy that the Government's action about wages was confined to the public sector'.[21] Since then the process has been taken several stages further, ending in a permanent Commission to report on methods of fixing wages and settling disputes in the state sector. In Italy too, 'the chief instrument of the state's pressure with regard to wage growth is the state's wages policy vis-à-vis its own employees and the employees of the nationalized industries in general'.[22]

Another well-rehearsed method is the threat of severe unemployment – not as a product of blind circumstance but as a consequence of policy. With unemployment at unusually high levels in Britain, Holland, Germany or Sweden in the early months of 1967, there are examples for the picking. Britain's is perhaps the clearest. When the Government introduced its wage freeze in July 1966, it was clearly not in response to any worsening of the internal economic situation – the economy was already faltering under the deflationary load of the preceding eighteen months, and the Chancellor had declared himself satisfied with the way things were going only a few weeks previously – but in panic reaction to pressure on the pound. We might never know how real the panic was: on the one hand a special dollar credit extended by the US in September 1965 and a package provided by the Central Banks the following June were nowhere near being exhausted; on the other, 'it had also been apparent for a long time that there was going to be little hope of reviving confidence in the Pound so long as the incomes policy had the appearance of being a bad economic joke'.[23] Real or not the Government wanted the

21. Fellner *et al.*, op. cit., p. 62.

22. Vittorio Foa, Deputy Secretary General, CGIL, 'Incomes Policy: A Crucial Problem for the Unions', *ISJ*, June 1964, p. 260.

23. C. Gordon Tether, 'Was That Big Stampede Really Necessary?' *Financial Times*, 19 September 1966.

unions to comply – and quickly. To this end Wilson warned the TUC that any breaking of ranks would be punished by severe unemployment – not the half-million he had previously envisaged or the million predicted by economists, but two million.[24] When the TUC bowed, the Government upped its demands beyond what was immediately required: R. H. S. Crossman, Leader of the House, warned the union leaders to prepare for the end of collective bargaining. Although quickly muffled and tempered the warning was repeated at all levels of government – 'nothing can be quite the same again'[25] became a Ministerial refrain. One Minister, Douglas Houghton, went so far as to envisage 'direction of labour in order to get our essential industries properly manned'[26] (to which Labour Party headquarters quickly added 'which, of course, would be un-thinkable in peace time', but not so quickly as to erase the impression that it had been both thinkable and expressed publicly).

The same intentions lie behind the proliferation of legal controls over labour. In Britain, a judgement in the House of Lords in 1964 – Rookes *v.* Barnard – 'knocked the bottom out of the certainty of the right to strike and to take other in-dustrial action' which had prevailed for nearly sixty years. Nor has that bottom been replaced. Despite its election pro-mises, Labour's 1965 Trades Disputes Act left 'unprotected many new areas of liability that were opened up by the judge-ments of 1964'.[27] Further restrictions came with the Prices and Incomes Act, 1966, which looks likely – at the time of writing – to remain permanently on the statute book in some form.[28] In Germany, the constitutionally-guaranteed right to organize has

24. At his meeting with the Economic Committee of the TUC, 25 July 1966.

25. William Rodgers, Parliamentary Under-Secretary at the Department of Economic Affairs, *Financial Times*, 21 September 1966.

26. Speaking at Doncaster, 29 October 1966, *The Times*, 31 October 1966.

27. K. W. Wedderburn, *The Worker and the Law*, Penguin, 1965, pp. 273–4, 293. Confirmed as regards the Act in private correspondence.

28. [It has; and has been strengthened by the Industrial Relations Act of 1969.]

been progressively narrowed by new union–employer bye-laws introducing 'automatic procedures which must be exhausted before a strike vote can be held'[29] and pressure has been growing throughout the sixties to enact a *Notstandsgesetz* (Emergency Law) that would give the Government full discretion in limiting trade union rights, in directing labour and so forth in the event of an imprecisely-defined emergency. It is almost certain that the 'grand' SPD–CDU Coalition will pass such legislation before it runs its course.[30] In Denmark, the very elaborate legal provisions against all strikes by state employees and unofficial strikes by all workers were further extended from 1956 onwards to cover particular wage awards and in 1963 to include all the provisions of the 'stabilization plan'. In the Netherlands, as befits the home of wages planning, legislation is total: all collective agreements, whose terms 'must be within the framework of the various statutory regulations regarding not only wage rates but also paid holidays, pensions and other fringe benefits, working conditions, etc.', become legally binding once approved by the central authorities.[31] In Belgium, where the most far-reaching amendments to the penal code proposed in 1962 were blocked by the unions, the Government has nonetheless armed itself with powers to requisition striking workers, and to impose heavier penalties for impeding communications and transport. In France and Italy, too, the legislative net has been tightened to distinguish between permissible and unofficial industrial action, the one sanctioned by the trade unions and hemmed in with notice-giving clauses, the other not.

There is no denying these methods some effectiveness either as blackmail or simply in providing union leaders with a convincing alibi. But their use is limited. Holding a wage line in the public sector appears discriminatory and is fought as

29. OEEC Secretariat, 'Wage Determination in Germany', in Fellner *et al.*, op. cit., p. 318.

30. [The *Notstandsgesetz* finally became law on 28 June 1968.]

31. OEEC Secretariat, 'Wage Determination in the Netherlands', in Fellner *et al.*, op. cit., p. 362.

such unless it is part of a general deflation. Deflation itself is costly. And legislation, as even the war-time record shows, is something of a paper tiger: 'in the last resort', the British Ministry of Labour pointed out to the Royal Commission on Trades Unions, 'it is not practicable, nor would it be conducive to good industrial relations, to try and put a large number of people in gaol'.[32]

Given the weaknesses of compulsion the wooing of the union leaders has been accompanied by a propagandist big beat seldom equalled in peace-time. *Consensus*, the achievement of a widespread, voluntary agreement that wage restraint is both necessary and beneficial, is the key to success and increasingly recognized as such. The authors of *The Problem of Rising Prices* were unequivocal about it in 1961.[33] 'In our kind of societies', echoed an OECD working party the following year, 'a successful incomes policy must derive its ultimate sanction from the understanding and cooperation of all those concerned.'[34] Signature of the *Statement of Intent* in Britain, the first formal step towards an agreed wages policy, was hailed by its author as 'a victory for the nation as a whole, a demonstration to the world that the British people are still prepared to respond to the needs of the country in peace-time no less than in war-time'.[35]

This is not entirely ballyhoo. The need for a 'consensus' on wages policy fits the overall tendency of modern capitalism to extend its domination beyond workers' behaviour to their motivations, beyond their activity in the workplace to their lives as a whole. For the trade union machine it is a condition of full integration in society without loss of power. For established

32. Royal Commission on Trade Unions and Employers' Organizations, 'Written Evidence of the Ministry of Labour', p. 7, quoted in T. Cliff and C. Barker, *Incomes Policy, Legislation and Shop Stewards* (London): London Industrial Shop Stewards' Defence Committee (1966), pp. 114–15. Chapter 8 of the booklet ('Anti-Union Legislation') contains a full discussion of the problem as seen in Britain.

33. loc. cit., pp. 56, 58, *passim*.

34. OECD, *Policies for Price Stability*, Paris, 1962.

35. George Brown, then Secretary of State for Economic Affairs, quoted in *The Times*, 17 December 1964.

society it is important enough for apparently far-reaching concessions to have been made to get it.

One of these has been to extend restriction to cover all types of income. In the early discussions there was little attempt to disguise wages policies or to call them by any other name. But the closer they come to implementation the more insistent become the calls for equality of sacrifice. 'If wage increases were to be limited in the way proposed' [by Fellner and his colleagues], demanded the Joint Trade Union Advisory Committee to the OEEC, 'then other types of income increases would also have to be limited.' [36] Within three years the OECD as such was suggesting that 'more thought should be given to the possible need for – and feasibility of – exerting more direct influence over the rise in other kinds of income', not only because of their impact on prices but for 'more general political and social considerations'.[37] Even as good a friend of his government as George Meany, President of the American Federation of Labour-Congress of Industrial Organizations reacted in that vein to the call for wage restraint. 'We are,' he said, 'prepared to sacrifice as much as anyone else for as long as anyone else as long as there is equality of sacrifice.' [38]

Within the basic premise of established ideology – that the economy is a national partnership between capital and labour in which strict symmetry of power prevails – it is a natural demand. Given the asymmetry that prevails in practice it is bound to be disappointed. Attempts to restrain profits by price control run up against problems of defining the vast majority of goods and making them stick to their definition; of intruding into the privacy of many non-labour costs; of reaching the hosts of individuals and institutions responsible for setting

36. 'Some JTUAC Comments on the Report of the Group of Experts on the Problem of Rising Prices', *Trade Union Affairs*, No. 4, Autumn–Winter 1961, p. 102.

37. *The Problems of Profits and Other Non-Wage Incomes*, Second Report on Policies for Price Stability by Working Party No. 4, Economic Policy Committee, Paris, OECD, February 1964, substantially reprinted in *Trade Union Affairs*, No. 6, Summer 1964, pp. 67, 72.

38. Quoted in *Financial Times*, 2 August 1966.

prices; of adjusting to exogenous factors like import prices; of finding other flexible indicators of changes in demand and economic power; and other influences on the allocation of resources. (Planning might have compromised the absolute power of price, it has not eliminated it entirely.)

Attempts to restrain profits directly through taxation run into even greater difficulties. Besides incidental problems like the ease with which they can be transmuted into 'costs' (expenses, fees and so on) by book-keeping manipulation, or the sheer lack of statistics, there are fundamental conceptual and institutional problems. Profits are a residual income, the *result* of economic activity, and also the major indicator of performance for both the individual firm and the economy as a whole. If the system is to work, and to be seen to work, as is being increasingly required by the spread of other controls, the movement of profits must remain flexible. They are also the fund for investment and competitive growth. To limit them is to head off the expanding firms and sectors and blunt the economy's competitive edge. The same could well be said of profit-control through limiting size (anti-monopoly action).

These are not academic difficulties. While blanket price and profit controls have been imposed at one time or another in peace-time in most countries, most recently in Denmark and France in 1963, or Britain in 1966, they have quickly eroded in practice. In the Danish case they were officially repealed after seven months; in France they resulted in 'a stagnation of investment which has got the economists in the national plan office extremely worried': [39] in Britain the market quickly bulldozed them aside so that within three months after the official standstill there was 'no doubt that prices have been increasing across the board'.[40]

In practice what starts out as profit control invariably ends as dividend limitation which is neither fully effective (since it can be avoided by issuing shares to existing owners through 'split' or 'rights' issues and other methods) nor to the point (since dividends are not coextensive with business incomes, nor

39. *Economist*, 6 August 1966, p. 581.
40. *Economist*, 3 September 1966, p. 937.

'income' as defined for tax purposes the only form of return on capital). And as even this marginal discrimination in favour of established firms and sectors conflicts with the overriding pursuit of growth since the well-established are not usually the fastest growing, it too is adopted gingerly and as a temporary measure.

It is clear that the search for equal sacrifice leads through craggy and inhospitable territory, in which the initial assumptions of social symmetry and common interest begin to be questioned. An interesting example occurred during the British price freeze of mid-1966. In an effort to avoid overwhelming the administration, the Department of Economic Affairs asked the Purchasing Officers' Association, organizer of 7,100 'buying executives' throughout industry, to report confidentially on price movements. The arrangement 'revealed price movements more quickly than any previous system', in the words of the Association's Director, but it also raised a number of fears. 'Is it right to do this?' questioned the *Financial Times*. 'It does seem slightly odd for a professional association to be used as "the eyes and ears of a government department" ... one is left with the uneasy feeling that the Purchasing Officers' Association is using its position in a way which goes beyond the normal functions of a professional association.' [41] What the reaction might have been had the 'eyes and ears' been an ordinary trade union, and had it been asked to report on management practices in general can be left to the imagination. The point is that any attempt to extend control beyond wages invokes the spectre of control by wage-earners. As the OECD suggested fairly early on, 'the implementation of a prices or incomes policy may conflict with other objectives of general economic and social policy'.[42] They were not wrong: prices policies presume a classless society; 'other objectives' normally do not.

By and large, union leaders have recognized the conflict and thought to resolve it politically, by attaching themselves to social democracy (or, in some cases, communism). In practice this attachment has been crucial in clinching and sustaining

41. *Financial Times*, 2 September 1966.
42. *The Problem of Prices*, loc. cit., p. 95.

wages policies; as crucial as wages policies have been in social
democracy's assumption and retention of office. In the Scandinavian countries, the partnership – under some strain now –
has been going more or less for a generation. In Holland, the
Labour Party's membership of the governing coalition follows
fairly closely the cycle of union acceptance and rejection of
current wages policies. In Britain, Labour's assumption of office
in 1964 owed as much to the unions' compliance with the intended wages policy as *vice versa*. Even in Italy despite the
situation being ostensibly so different, the same pulls can be
seen. The CGIL, which opposes wages policies, 'refuses integration with the state, and aims at a situation of dual power
that would gradually render impossible capitalist methods of
managing the economy and society',[43] is forced in practice to
operate within the existing institutional framework. It is still
officially opposed to working within the national administration but it has agreed to debate Italy's first Five Year Plan,
albeit 'piecemeal', and has demanded participation in the
emerging organs of the Common Market. Given that a substantial minority of the CGIL leadership is attached to a
member party of the governing 'Centre-Left' coalition, and
that its policy towards the supranational organizations – ob-
struction or participation – has never been made clear, the
current seepage towards parliamentarism within the CGIL is
almost bound to swell into a flood.

The union leaders' acceptance of wages planning is not an
end in itself. They must also be able to make wages policy
work. And here the record is sobering. Turner and Zoetewij
conclude from their survey of the results in a number of
countries that 'the limit of a temporary reduction in real wages
seems unlikely to exceed five per cent and the period of a wage
freeze about one year', and that such periods are more likely
to be followed by 'an explosive "dam break"' than by a
'gradual wage thaw'. As for the long-term course of wages, 'the
degree of wage stability that can be hoped for from a system
of central wage regulation in a mixed economy with free trade

43. Jean-Marie Vincent, 'Blick auf die italienischen Gewerkschaften',
Arbeitshefte, Duisburg, Jg. 2, Nr 4/5 p. 14.

unions is limited'.[44] Econometric studies for Britain chime in neatly. Reviewing a number of them, one commentator concludes: '*at most* the effect of trade unions in the post-war period has been to slow down the growth of nationally negotiated wage rates, particularly in the late forties during the period of wage restraint. Their effect on actual hourly earnings . . . was negligible.'[45] And even in Holland, 'the share of labour in the national income . . . has not been much influenced by the system of wage determination, and has, as in other industrialized countries, been largely determined by the complex of economic and political forces governing the level of employment and the incidence of taxation'.[46]

Behind the detail lies the need, if wages policies are to work, for society as a whole to achieve a consensus about the distribution of income. And although the union leaderships have been allowed every concession to help corral their membership into that consensus, from nominal autonomy in policy-making (the 'voluntary principle') to 'intermittent relaxation' in wages planning and legislative backing for their authority, it remains as elusive as ever.

44. Turner and Zoetewij, op. cit., pp. 135, 144.

45. Bob Rowthorne, 'The Trap of an Incomes Policy', *New Left Review*, 34, November–December 1965, p. 6.

46. O E E C Secretariat, 'Wage Determination in the Netherlands', in Fellner *et al.*, op. cit., p. 389.

6. Politics

The old civil servant watched the new Minister studying a file. 'I think I ought to warn you, Sir,' he said, 'that we don't take that organization very seriously.'

'I think I ought to warn you,' said the Minister amiably, 'that I am a member of this organization.'
The Times, 30 November 1964

Until the Labour Party came to office in Britain in 1964, the trade unions would have nothing to do with a wages policy. They have since accepted one. Until then no major legislation had been laid on the unions for almost forty years. Among the new Government's first acts was the appointment of a Royal Commission on Trade Unions and, for form's sake, Employers' Associations. It has since invoked emergency legislation to deal with strikes; imposed – by law – a wages freeze; announced the impending legislative euthanasia of collective bargaining; and reduced take-home pay over a wide range of industries. And still most unions concur, while the overwhelming majority of those that do not – like the Transport and General Workers' Union, whose General Secretary resigned from the Government on the issue – have precipitated no action against individual items of policy, let alone against the Government as such.

There is nothing peculiarly British in this. In Holland, the Labour Party was in office when twice the unions were made to accept wage cuts – March 1951 and June 1957. The Social Democrats were in the coalition that imposed the Stabilization Plan on Denmark in 1963. A Centre-Left government policed the Italian recession of 1964–5. And the Social-Democrat–Christian 'grand coalition' in Germany is set fair (1967) to introduce an extended series of anti-union Emergency Laws.[1]

The conjunction of Social Democracy and labour restraint is not surprising. It is natural to turn to the traditional reformist party in a crisis situation when reforms are clearly seen to be necessary. It is also natural for the powers that be to use Social Democracy consciously as a foil against more dangerous trends.

1. [These Laws were promulgated on 28 June 1968.]

It was, after all, from important sections of industry – Fiat, Montecatini, and many of the state corporations like ENI – that pressure came for the Centre-Left experiment in Italy in 1963, after a massive strike upheaval; it was the Confindustria (Confederation of Italian Industry) as a whole that reproved Christian Democrat 'snipers' for bringing about a crisis in the Moro–Nenni coalition in 1966.

By and large the unions have emerged from the storms with their social-democratic proclivities intact (see Chapter 5). What this means in terms of social consensus, how deeply the magic of 'our boys in Westminister' or 'in Bonn' or wherever penetrates the working population as a whole, remains to be seen.

Parliament

Parliamentary initiative and discretion have taken a hammering from the developments already outlined. International integration has reduced to a shadow the scope for truly national policies and this shadow is itself fixed in a complex of international treaty obligations. Nor is there much room domestically for policy manoeuvre. Leaving aside the irruption of mass working-class parties which has reduced debate to set confrontations between voting blocs defending decisions taken elsewhere, the size of the state sector and its committal of resources for years in advance nullifies most of what Parliament used to do in controlling the Government's purse-strings. Size in the private sector and state–private integration reduce Parliament's more general influence over the economy. Even planning, the instrument of social and economic control *par excellence*, has cramped its powers. Once national goals are set – and this is seldom done in open discussion; goals are seldom discussed at all except in terms of 'more' or 'less' – the means flow fairly automatically and need no parliamentary forum to discover their virtue. On the contrary, devotees of planning *and* parliamentary government are sufficiently worried about the seeming contradiction between the two to outline, at one end of the spectrum, 'fresh political techniques to secure the effective control of enlarged governmental power',[2] or to pronounce, at the other end, that the 'separation of economic and political institutions should be a fundamental principle of modern organization'.[3]

In Britain, the shrinkage of Parliament's role has been going on for a long time. A hundred years ago, Bagehot identified it as a shift from government by Parliament to government by Cabinet.[4] Recently, Crossman picked out a further shift to Prime Ministerial rule, based on the convergence on the Prime Minister's Office, during and since the war, of three power structures – the Civil Service, the mass party and the Cabinet.[5] Add to these an increasingly direct relationship between Prime Minister and electorate, serviced in one direction by the mass media – television especially – and, in the other, by public opinion polls, and we have a mechanism for executive government with little room for Parliament as such.

One result has been to impact Government and Opposition into each other programmatically and ideologically. In Britain the climate is normally one of implicit coalition, 'a climate', reports *The Times* Political Correspondent mournfully, nostalgic for the grand debate, the fun and mischievousness of genuine difference, 'in which Mr Heath feels as much obliged as Mr Wilson to say and do nothing that will give Washington, Paris or Bonn a jolt; in which Opposition leaders make (as a backbench Tory knight of long experience says) "committee stage speeches", full of facts and ratiocination, when they ought to be having a fling'.[6] It is a climate dignified academically as the 'law of convergence'; and one in which elections are fought increasingly on personality and presentation, not programme or policy: Mr Wilson's youth, pipe and raincoat *v*. Mr Heath's

2. Shonfield, op. cit., p. 388. Part 4 of the book is devoted to 'An Essay on some Political Implications of Active Government'.

3. Firmin Oulès, *Economic Planning and Democracy*, Penguin, 1966, p. 357.

4. Walter Bagehot, *The English Constitution*, first published in book form in 1867.

5. Introduction to Walter Bagehot, *The English Constitution*, Collins, Fontana Library, 1963.

6. *The Times*, 1 July 1966.

youth, yacht and choir practice; one set of market researchers against another.

On the Continent, reflecting an even narrower range of national options and a different tradition, the coalition is almost everywhere explicit, in intention if not in fact. In Germany, the 'grand' SPD–CDU coalition jelled at last in 1966. In Holland, Belgium, Austria, the Scandinavian countries and Italy, social democratic parties have been members of coalitions for most of the period since the war.

Parliamentary effectiveness has withered pitifully in consequence. In Britain, where the Commons still controls the purse in theory and spends one third of its sitting-time on finance, the last occasion it rejected a Government Estimate – on MP's travelling allowances – was in 1921; and government expenditure has gone up and up and up. Huge outlays – like the £100 million initial commitment to nuclear weapons – have been hidden from it, in that case agreed on the nod as expenditure on 'research'. And ever since 1962, when the presentation of the Civil Estimates was changed, it has been denied the means of scrutiny. And so it is from the great decisions on war and peace – whether those connected with nuclear weapon production, the Suez invasion, or support for the US war in Vietnam (which has not yet been debated as such in Congress) to the little ones about timing the opening of Parliament to coincide with Lord Home's metamorphosis into plain Sir Alec, or announcing the name of the new Ombudsman months before the legislation creating his job could become law, or holding fast to a pound–decimal system because administrative decisions had already been taken – Parliament has no right to know or to decide. As Wilson told his supporters, murmuring under the strain of the Government's Vietnam policy, 'I cannot keep you posted on these delicate diplomatic issues from week to week. I cannot keep the House of Commons posted from week to week. The responsibilities of Government do not allow that.' [7]

Denied power and insulted for the lack of it, Parliament's independence has given way to tetchiness and a querulous

7. *The Times* report of a Parliamentary Labour Party meeting, 7 July 1966.

concern with Speakers' rulings, parliamentary reform, rebuilding and televising – an altogether disproportionate concern with Parliament itself rather than its milieu.

It is an atmosphere unlikely to reverse the withdrawal of public interest. In Britain, average daily sales of Hansard declined from 8,889 in 1954 to 2,359 in 1966; the tone of parliamentary reporting in the posh papers has become increasingly light and mannered – a chronicle of curiosities, rather than a record of important events; and the reading public has a library of criticism to choose from, including *The Passing of Parliament, Can Parliament Survive?, Parliament in Danger!, Has Parliament a Future?, What's Wrong with Parliament?, Parliament and Mumbo-Jumbo, Change or Decay,* and a lot more in the same vein.

More important, Parliament is increasingly by-passed by the big lobbies. Business interests 'do not fight each other to get their men in Parliament. They seem to be content with a general situation which gives to business as a whole a stake'.[8] As for the unions which created the Labour Party specifically to secure parliamentary representation, and which thought at the time 'that the great battles between capital and labour are to be fought out on the floor and in the division lobbies of the Houses of Commons' – they too have 'ceased to see in Parliament more than a shield or a platform for the defence of their general interests', and 'a reward for long years of uncomplaining service' on the part of their officers.[9]

Most important of all is the growing estrangement between politics and voting. In Britain, where turnout during general elections has been consistently high at seventy-five to eighty per cent of the electorate since the war, 'political attitudes coincide only to a limited extent with party images and voting behaviour'.[10] They have more to do with membership of a trade union, home environment and even religion. Moreover, political agnosticism is spreading: in 1951, twenty per cent of

8. Blondel, op. cit., p. 222.

9. Robert Dowse, 'Trade Union MPs in Opposition', *Trade Union Affairs*, Summer 1964, p. 37.

10. Blondel, op. cit., p. 87.

people thought that it mattered little or not at all which party was in power; by 1959 the proportion had grown to thirty-eight per cent;[11] and by 1964 to forty-nine per cent.[12] In the circumstances it is not surprising that changes in government hinge on the course of abstention rather than on participation;[13] that 471 seats in the Commons – or nearly three quarters of the total – are considered to be 'safe' whatever the policies at issue; and that critics of established bipartisan assumptions make so little headway at the polls whether they champion causes in which the electorate is more radical than Parliament (wage freeze or Vietnam, for example) or more conservative (homosexual law reform or corporal punishment, for example).

In other countries voting behaviour is even more conditioned by environmental factors – religion often plays a larger part and political involvement is even lower. In Germany, a 1959 survey of 'vestigial Marxism in the conceptual world of industrial workers' for the Deutsches Industrie-Institut, found that forty-five per cent were either indifferent to, or completely uninterested in, parliamentary representation.[14] In Italy, to judge from the constant barrage of press criticism, 'parliament, the fortress of democracy' is merely a place for the 'growing abandonment of men to abstraction and indifference ... [and to] the mystique of rules, the cult of tactical ability and personal fortunes'.[15] In France, the average citizen's attitude to the General's conduct of affairs, is 'that of open-mouthed and rapt spectators watching a gifted conjurer pulling increasingly large rabbits out of his *képi*. They applaud, they do not feel involved.'[16]

11. David Butler and Richard Rose, *The British General Election of 1959*, London, Macmillan, 1960, p. 19.

12. David Butler and Anthony King, *The British General Election of 1964*, London, Macmillan; New York, St Martin's Press, 1965, p. 115.

13. See the pioneer study by R. S. Milne and H. C. Mackenzie, *Marginal Seat, 1955 (Bristol North-East)*, Hansard Society for Parliamentary Government, 1958.

14. Heinz Theo Risse, 'Abhängigkeit und Freiheit' in Marianne Feuersenger (ed.), *Gibt es Noch ein Proletariat?*, Frankfurt/Main, Europäische Verlaganstalt, 1962, p. 72.

15. *La Stampa*, Turin, 6 October 1966.

16. *The Times* Paris Correspondent, 28 August 1966.

The ebb is not without its waves of political interest, as during the course of the presidential elections in France; but they are becoming shorter and weaker. For the electorate knows, and the Minister for Scientific Research has admitted (and denied) that, 'everything has changed since the election of the President of the Republic by universal suffrage. He is the source of power, and power is derived from him. He embodies national legitimacy. If peradventure the [Gaullist] majority became the minority, the government would not be entrusted to the Oppositions.'[17] And, as if to back him up, the marginally victorious Gaullist government assumed plenary powers (Summer 1967) to cope with an altogether unexceptional bout of economic stagnation and social protest.

Given the constraints on Parliament everywhere, it is difficult not to see in Paris the political writing on the wall for the entire West.

Declining Welfare State

An important corollary of Parliament's decline and a big factor in the withdrawal of mass political interest is its decreasing relevance for the attainment of direct, felt reforms.

There are two aspects here. On the one hand, the balance of state-provided social security benefits and costs has shifted against the working population and its dependents since the mid-fifties.[18] On the other for the majority of workers, state-provided benefits have yielded pride of place as a prop to living standards to private fringe-benefits. In 1960, these amounted to thirteen to fourteen per cent of wages in British industry,[19]

17. M. Alain Peyrefitte, reported in *The Times*, 22 February 1967.

18. See R. J. Nicholson, 'The Distribution of Personal Income', *Lloyds Bank Review*, January 1967, pp. 11–21; 'The incidence of taxes and social service benefits in 1963 and 1964', *Economic Trends*, August 1966, pp. ii–xxii, and earlier articles under similar titles in ibid., November 1962, February 1964.

19. G. L. Reid and D. J. Robertson, 'The Cost of Fringe Benefits in British Industry', in Reid and Robinson (eds.), op. cit., Chapter 3, and 'Conclusions', ibid., p. 314.

compared with welfare 'benefit expenditure' at 12·6 per cent of consumer outlay.[20] While there is no way of directly comparing the two items for earlier years, a lot of circumstantial evidence points to the steady drift of welfare from public to private provenance: by early 1966 it was estimated that twelve million employees, half the total, were covered by private occupational pension schemes, and that the number was increasing by half-a-million a year; between 1948 and 1965, the three largest of the private health-insurance schemes increased their membership 1,300 per cent;[21] and pressure – not entirely middle-class – to contract out of state education and health is growing.[22]

The relative importance of state welfare is not declining for everyone. The utterly poor – pensioners, the ill, the slow, members of large families and victims of broken ones – are still as utterly dependent on the state. For them there are few if any private benefits to temper the wind of public avarice. But for the mass of workers there is now at least the shadow of a choice.

Direct welfare is not the whole story. Parliament is losing its reformist lustre in a wider sense too. In the early years of working-class parliamentary politics the balance of protection and suppression, however erratic, seemed generally tilted towards the underprivileged. In Britain, the Liberal Reforms of 1906–11 protected the right to strike, permitted trade unions to finance political activity, introduced school meals, pensions and unemployment pay as well as payment for M Ps. While far less daring, the Labour Governments of 1945–51 nonetheless reasserted the trade unions' political freedoms, established the National Health Service and extended the public sector. But 1964 changed all that. The legislative pendulum has not ceased to hammer workers and their organizations ever since.

20. ILO, *The Cost of Social Security, 1958–1960*, Geneva, 1964, Part II, Table 4, p. 249.
21. *The Times*, 27 January 1966.
22. See Ralph Harris and Arthur Seldon, *Choice in Welfare 1965*, London, Institute of Economic Affairs Ltd, 1965, Part V *passim*. Tendentious but illuminating.

The Government's 'forward policy' – the phrase is Ray Gunter's, then Minister of Labour – has permitted ministers to anticipate strikes by public warnings to those involved, to incite the general public against workers in dispute, to call on managers to be firm in dealing with labour, to announce the end of collective bargaining. It has upheld a colour bar in immigration, strengthened the House of Lords, and shown timidity bordering on paralysis in matters of individual freedom. There is no hint of wobble in the way the balance is now tilted.

It is foolhardy to generalize about parliamentary history, particularly when international parallels are sought. But what else can be made of the transition from the reformist upsurge of the Weimar Republic in Germany to the looming *Notstandsgesetz*; from Blum to de Gaulle in France; from the advances during the thirties in the Scandinavian countries to the parliamentary sclerosis affecting the area today – if not the outlines of the same switch from protection to discipline? There are exceptions. As in many things, the US's basic economic strength provides some shelter from the prevailing economic wind, and a few small reforms – the poverty programme, Medicare, Civil Rights, city survival – are seeping through. In almost every national parliament it is possible to point to some legislation for the underprivileged, as it is possible to point everywhere to the continuing value of existing welfare provisions. But the overall tendency is to drain from Parliament its reformist sponsorship.

The same goes for the petty-reformist and welfare activities of local government. The trend everywhere is towards a tautening of social and economic administration and their centralization. Civil Rights in the US are merely the latest to have clashed with, and weakened, States' Rights; and urban administration is increasingly locked in Federal controls over housing, 'renewal' or highways. In Germany the *Länder* are being compelled to increase their tax transfusions to the Centre and limit their autonomy in spending. Italy's 'structural reforms' are aimed as much at shaping local authorities to national purposes as at anything else.

Working-Class Parties

It would be unusual for these developments not to have forced a number of adjustments on the mass working-class parties. Most of them have simply resiled from reformist positions. They are content to administer what is and ignore what might be. Normally, the change has been projected as an advance from doctrinalism to pragmatism: from the narrow, selfish and dated concern with class to a more responsible appreciation of the needs of the nation as a whole; from Marx to Keynes. Advance or retreat, both Social Democracy and Communism have shifted, the one from a total and exclusive commitment to Parliament as the mainspring of social change to a total and exclusive commitment to Parliament *tout court*, the other from denying 'the parliamentary road to socialism' to adopting it.

In the British Labour Party, the least ideological of them all, the shift has been the most confused and interrupted. Only after the electoral defeat of 1955 and as part of the post-mortem on it did the party leadership take to illuminating their strategy in theoretical terms. In two pamphlets – *Socialism and Nationalization* and *Recent Developments in British Socialist Thinking* – Hugh Gaitskell concentrated on discounting nationalization and promoting government economic management as a means of social control. The Socialist Union through their monthly journal *Socialist Commentary* backed him.[23] C. A. R. Crosland generalized his leader's identification with society – now called 'post-capitalist' – in *The Future of Socialism*; and John Strachey got his and his colleagues' quietus of Marx in *Contemporary Capitalism*. All of these were published in 1956. The following year, with the policy pamphlet *Industry and Society*, the Labour Party officially affirmed its own identification: 'large firms' it declared, 'are as a whole serving the nation well'; instead of nationalizing private industry it proposed to privatize public funds through the purchase by Government of a non-controlling interest in 'the 600'.

23. See particularly Part B of the Socialist Union's manifesto, *Twentieth Century Socialism*, Penguin, 1956.

The next electoral defeat (1959) triggered a ferocious attack on the party's untidy ideological baggage. At that year's Conference, Gaitskell hung the results at the polls on the most famous clause in the party's Constitution, the only one to adorn every member's card – Clause 4 which, calls *inter alia*, for 'the common ownership of the means of production, distribution and exchange' – and demanded its deletion. This time, however, the party's lack of doctrine came to the defence of tradition, and the baggage was retained.

That was the end of the first and only open attempt to refocus Labour's view of its role in society. Since then the process has gone on gradually, on individual issues, without theoretical illumination, so that the party is still ostensibly dedicated to securing 'for the workers by hand or by brain the full fruits of their industry and the most equitable distribution thereof', while actually dispensing from its position in government wage cuts, unemployment and restrictive legislation on a scale unknown since before the war. The process has gone on, not as a debate on principle but as an assertion by the parliamentary party of its independence from the party, its annual policy-making Conference and its Executive; and as a rapid attenuation of the parliamentary party's control over its leaders, (the backbencher, poor soul, has now gone the full gamut from 'normal consultation' before and during the war, through Attlee's Liaison Committee – 'more a watchdog for the government than a lever of pressure upon it'[24] – to the current régime of insult and abuse). In its Wilsonian version, the most emphatic to date, the party's Constitution reads: 'The Government must govern, and must be seen to govern.'

Ideology is taken more seriously on the Continent, and so the break has generally been more obvious and thorough. In Germany, the crucial moment came in 1959, at the SPD's Bad Godesberg Congress, when public ownership was solemnly dropped and the dilute Marxism of Shumacher's 'socialist people's party' made way for the equally dilute Keynesianism of the current 'people's party'. In Italy the process stretched over four congresses of the PSI (1959–65) during which the

24. Miliband, op. cit., p. 296.

Nenni leadership guided the party from common action and a shared perspective with the Communist Party to, first, support – 'from outside' – of a Centre-Left coalition of Christian Democrats and (Right) Social Democrats, then to participation in a broader Centre-Left (1963) and finally (1966) to reunification – after nineteen years – with the (Right) Social Democrats. In Sweden the move was made as early as 1944; in Belgium in 1950; Austria in 1956. In one Social Democratic party after another the break with a reformist tradition under the guise of a break with (Marxist) dogma has more or less been accomplished since the war.

It has not come easily. In each case the leadership has had to shift a mound of history to gain their freedom from policy; in each case it has had to find alternatives for uncomplicated principles which, if nothing else, provided common coordinates for the largely self-organized membership; and it has had to do so under fire from a Left exasperated in defence of these principles, and without the close cover it had come to expect from the trade-union leadership. In practice, it has tried to fill the ideological void with discipline and to substitute a professional, paid force for the enthusiastic volunteers of its reformist heyday.

Abroad both the battles and the casualties have been more apparent than in Britain. In Italy, the PSI's final abandonment of opposition led some of its most active workers to break away to form the PSIUP (Italian Socialist Party of Proletarian Unity) which, within two months of its founding, was claiming 150,000 members, twenty-five parliamentary deputies and thirteen Senators.[25] More important in the long run, though much slower to be felt, has been the decline in PSI influence in the major trade union federation, the CGIL. In Belgium, a complex of issues and events rooted in the massive general strike four years earlier resulted in the first cluster of breakaways to the Left in 1965, and a sharp decline in activity – as later seen in the electoral returns – on the part of those that remained. In Norway, Social Democracy has splintered leftwards, suffering

25. Lelio Basso, 'A New Socialist Party', *International Socialist Journal* No. 2, April 1964, pp. 171, 173.

a decline in activity and losing heavily at the polls this decade. In Denmark it failed to benefit from the splits in the Communist Party.[26] And even in Germany, where for long it managed to preserve a heavy-handed monolithism, the run up to the first post-coalition election has brought the first cracks in the party.

Official Social Democracy has not suffered as much as might have been expected. Its own Left critics almost everywhere confined the attack to its *parliamentary* policy, pressed it to undertake classic, *state-granted* reforms, to adapt the system in favour of the working class through *legislation* – acted, in short, on the assumption of Parliament's freedom to manoeuvre. In some cases, the assumption was held fairly critically. First in Belgium, then in Italy, the Social Democratic Left rallied to a slogan of 'structural reforms' conceived as 'an aspect of a total socialist strategy motivated by a conscious desire to conduct a revolutionary action within capitalist society and therefore sustained by a permanent effort on the part of the working class'.[27] But even where the slogan retains some vitality – and this is not everywhere so: the Belgian Socialist Party, for example, holds it in common with its Left critics – it is inevitably formulated in more specific and embracing terms politically than industrially, and as inevitably, given the non-revolutionary background on to which it is projected, focuses attention on parliamentary action, no matter how many and how earnest the warnings against doing just that.

Caught in this way between parliamentarism and parliament's rigidity, Left Social Democracy has suffered even more than the official variety. Its record of impotence under the pounding of the Labour Government in Britain needs no comment. But even where it is unhampered by office, it is

26. [And fell – in February 1968 – to a 'bourgeois' coalition government. Swedish Social Democracy's surprise victory at the polls in September that year was due almost entirely to popular reaction against the Russian invasion of Czechoslovakia.]

27. Lelio Basso, 'Old Contradictions and New Problems', *International Socialist Journal* No. 15, July 1966, p. 253.

rarely more credible. In France it exists nationally by clinging to the fraying coat-tails of the Communist Party; in Germany, even before the Coalition it scarcely existed at all; in Italy, Belgium or Scandinavia it is reduced to seeking a role rather than acting one out.

The crisis has not spared the Communist Parties. Cut loose from their 'Russian alternative' since the onset of organized de-Stalinization, they have both embraced parliament and – so far – been rejected, and so have managed to contract the disease of Social Democracy without gaining the balm of office. The results are to be seen throughout the western Communist world in splits – often under the guise of 'Maoist' breakaways – and in the official parties' immobilism and defensiveness.

Politics in the Working Class

These developments have taken their toll of working-class involvement and interest. In turn, the dwindling working-class presence has left the political leaderships free to make whatever programmatic changes they felt necessary, and stronger in their assault on the Left's defensive positions. The tensions caused by the changes, the subsequent loss in direction by both leadership and Left, the attendant disciplinary measures and splits and the heat generated over evident trifles have done a great deal more to lessen workers' active concern with their traditional parties.

Something has already been said about the official trade union view of Parliament's efficiency. While on balance their ties are still with the traditional working-class parties, this is not always so; and where it is, it is less meaningful now that there are other, more direct ways of influencing policy. In Britain, although the Labour Party still receives the bulk of its central funds in contributions from the unions, these have consistently fallen short of expenditure since 1950, except for one year – 1955. Union payments into the party's election fund have been highly erratic, up from 1945 to 1950, down for the election of 1951, down further for 1955, up slightly for 1959, up again – dramatically – for 1964, and down again for 1966.

The National Council of Labour on which representatives of the Labour Party, the TUC and the Cooperative Union meet formally has fallen into desuetude. Most important of all, the possibility of a break with the party, unthinkable for so long, has actually been mooted, at the very highest level.[28]

In Germany, where the unions as such are not affiliated to the SPD and where both major parties have large trade-union offices, 'the trade unionists' traditional fraternal-socialist trust for Social Democracy has been weakened by the formation of unitary trade unions and by the party's most recent course. It still exists on a personal level – as for example the relationship between the older generation of trade-union leaders and Erich Ollenhauer. But this older generation is retiring on both sides . . .'[29]

In Italy, pressure is mounting to abolish political elections within the trade-union federations as many of the leaders, in the CGIL particularly, draw back from their party associations. In France, where the Communist Party has managed to retain tight control of the major trade-union federation – the CGT – it has simply lost members, from nearly six million in 1947 to about a million today. And so too, in Belgium, Holland and, no doubt, elsewhere.

Mounting reservations amongst trade-union leaders are only part of the story, and not the most important. None of the mass parties is an exclusive spokesman for its class: the Labour Party in Britain commands electoral support from about two

28. Most recently by one of the General Secretaries of the National Graphical Association – John Bonfield. Writing in the union's journal, August 1967, he drew attention to the 'growing consciousness among trade unionists that this is not "our government" in the sense that previous Labour Governments were – by virtue of their basic sympathy with trade union aims and aspirations', and remarked on the consequence that 'trade unionists' were wondering whether they 'ought to continue to put their hands in their pockets to pay for it all' (quoted in *The Times*, 3 August 1967).

29. Peter von Oertzen, 'Wo steht der DGB?', *Arbeitshefte*, Jg. 2/3, Nr. 11/1, 20 February 1964, p. 44. As if to emphasize the point, Ollenhauer died soon after the article was written.

thirds of workers, while just over half the Conservative vote comes from them:[30] in Germany two thirds of the CDU vote is working-class compared with eighty-seven per cent for the SPD.[31] Yet they are all losing members from the peak figures reached soon after the war: in Britain, individual membership of the Labour Party has declined fairly steadily from over one million in 1953 to 800,000 in 1965; and since the minimum affiliation was raised more than threefold to 800 in 1957 a higher proportion than ever are the dead souls paid for by local parties in order to qualify. In the Italian Communist Party, membership declined from two and a half to one and a half million in the decade to 1966; and in France from 900,000 to about 350,000 between 1947 and 1966.

Declining membership has naturally tended to age the parties, perhaps not to the extent reported from Belgium, where the Brussels Socialist Federation of the Socialist Party showed an increase in its superannuated membership from ten per cent of the total in 1959 to twenty-four per cent in 1962, or where pensioners account for two fifths of the members in some sections under local Socialist administration,[32] but sufficiently to excite acid comment from most critics on the Left.

More important, it has helped to make the parties increasingly middle-class. It is true that the seemingly abstract nature of political activity has always tended to favour middle-class involvement, even in working-class parties; and that the organization of parties on residential rather than occupational lines has worked in the same direction. It is also true that working-class parties quickly attracted middle-class elements denied effective influence, such as the (anti-clerical) teachers in most of Catholic Europe; and that their growing power and their assumption of office nationally and locally attracted careerists of all classes, even where a party card was not a *de facto* requirement for public office. But the process has accelerated

30. Blondel, op. cit., p. 58.

31. Michael Vester, 'SPD und Arbeitnehmerpolitik – Zum Dortmunder Parteitag der SPD', *Arbeitshefte*, 15 July 1966, p. 26.

32. *La Gauche*, 14 December 1963, cited by Marcel Liebman, 'The Crisis of Belgian Social Democracy', *Socialist Register 1966*, p. 65.

tremendously since the war. In Britain, the proportion of working-class Labour parliamentary candidates (including trade-union officials) dropped from twenty-seven per cent of the total in 1951 to twenty-one per cent in 1966;[33] their concentration in safe seats has been seriously upset by the changing location of industry and the growing financial independence of many Constituency Labour Parties; and even trade-union sponsored candidates – working class in our definition – are increasingly middle class in fact: of the Transport and General Workers' twenty-seven sponsored M Ps in the current Parliament only seven 'are likely ever to have done a manual job', the rest include lawyers, teachers, a theatre director, a meteorologist and Anthony Greenwood. Of the Municipal and General's ten, 'not more than two would normally be thought of as typical members of the union'.[34] And what is true at the summit, is true too, although to a less degree, on the slopes: 'at every level, the working class and trade-union element is being undermined'.[35]

From Italy, the same picture. Even before socialist unification, workers were streaming out of the PSI and being replaced by 'civil servants and the employees in the semi-State companies'.[36] And in the Communist Party which closed down a third of its trade-union cells in the five years to 1962 and watched its working-class membership drop to a third of the total, the leadership continued to complain – May 1965 – that 'the percentage of workers among party members was diminishing and so was the number of workers who were active within the most industrialized areas'.[37] And so it is in the rest of Europe – the mass working-class parties are possessed by clerks.

33. From D. E. Butler, *The British General Election of 1951*, London, Macmillan, 1952, p. 41; D. E. Butler and Anthony King, *The British General Election of 1966*, London, Macmillan; New York, St Martin's Press, 1966, p. 209.

34. *The Times*, 15 July 1966.

35. Martin Harrison, op. cit., p. 268.

36. Lelio Basso, 'The Italian Left', *Socialist Register 1966*, p. 34.

37. *The Times*, 31 May 1965, reporting on a convention of Communist factory cadres.

Consensus

A decline in mass involvement is not automatically translated into declining votes. On the contrary, the major working-class parties in Europe enjoy solid and often growing electoral support.

One reason is that the environmental determinants of voting behaviour retain their effect long after the initial politics are abandoned. Although there are environmental influences acting in the opposite direction – migration from 'Labour' to 'Conservative' regions (in Britain from 'the North' to 'the South-east'), from urban concentrations to suburbs and new towns – they are generally less effective, since the weight of evidence points to trade union membership and, ultimately, concentration in large production units, as 'the most satisfactory single element in "explanation" of voting behaviour'.[38] Another reason is that increasing efficiency in propaganda and vote gathering (where voting it not compulsory) squeezes increasing advantage from these factors; and a third – which needs no repeating – is that voting is becoming less and less a serious business as the range of policy choice narrows.

So far these circumstances have helped the Social Democratic parties, hoisting them into office, keeping them there and making them look like the natural governing party in the west, 'the main support of the capitalist régime' or whatever, depending on the political vantage point of the observer. But even while these environmental influences continue to work themselves out, other developments – as yet no bigger than a man's hand – are gathering to swamp them.

Most important is the displacement of workers' traditional 'solidaristic collectivism', based on inherited social ties and values, by an 'instrumental collectivism' based on a rational and continuing calculation of self-interest.[39] The change itself is bound up with the growing mobility of workers both between jobs – one way or another three fifths of manufacturing jobs in Canada are terminated every year, in the US half, in France

38. Blondel, op. cit., p. 67.

39. The phrase is John H. Goldthorpe and David Lockwood's in 'Affluence and the British Class Structure', *Sociological Review*, July 1963.

about thirty-five per cent, Britain over a third, Germany thirty per cent – and from lower to higher grades – in Britain the proportion of white-collar workers in the economy as a whole is increasing three times as fast as between 1911 and 1931, one third faster than the 1931–51 rate, while in the US, white-collar employment is growing five times faster than manual employment; and although 'white-collar' is not synonymous with 'skilled' the two do grow in the same direction.

For the moment, organized 'instrumental' attitudes are to be seen only in isolated pockets in any national labour movement, clearest in the fast-growing white-collar unions, the most uninhibited and demanding of them all. But – as is shown in the next chapter – they are spreading. And while they can be very narrow, very selfish, indeed ugly, politically they do fasten on to a party's performance rather than its protestations, on to the present rather than the past. If they grow, as they seem bound to, traditional working-class parties will need to work hard to stay their current supporters' slipping loyalties.

This is easier said than done. If there is a single lesson to be drawn from this chapter it is that the parties are so firmly clasped in the rigidities of the system they would find it almost impossible to respond to the insistent, shifting demands of pork-barrel loyalty; so firmly, that they have had to insulate themselves from mass pressure in order to exist. And while this applies to all parties and so leads to their convergence on the political middle ground, which in turn leaves little room for voter mobility and fickleness; and while it further implies that the party in possession is unlikely to be turned out quickly or easily by rivals who are similar in so many respects, the very rigidities that keep it in office as a 'national consensus party' are bound eventually to make it lose touch with its electoral supporters. Under the circumstances, disenchantment is liable to be sudden and severe, reflecting the degree of organization of self-interest. It is difficult to see in any other light the erosion of Scandinavian and, perhaps, Belgian, Dutch and Austrian Social Democracy this decade; or to believe that younger Social Democrat leaders in Britain, Germany or Italy, where electoral expansion has probably still to reach its apogee do not consider their long-term prospects with a tinge of apprehension.

Meanwhile, though votes there be, they are more likely than not to obscure the workers' parties' declining real popular influence. As more people, particularly more working-class people, withdraw from active involvement in the parties' life and aims, fewer remain exposed to their moral authority and opinion-forming processes, and the momentary encounter at the polls becomes less and less meaningful. These might be ideal circumstances for the parties to adopt policies of wage-control and labour regulation, but they are hardly ideal for attaining the consensus on which these policies ultimately depend. On the contrary, in opting for them and so thrusting politics into the workplace, Social Democracy is contributing directly to that fusion of politics and economics in both aims and methods which it has always rightly feared as a violently unstable mixture.

7. Workers

Centralization

'If,' runs the authentic voice of union baronialism, 'the trade unions themselves are to surrender their authority [over wage claims], I suggest they ought to surrender it to this body and not to Government.'[1] And within a year they had, making over some of their autonomy to the TUC's wage-vetting machinery. In the US too, the combined Congress of Industrial Organizations–American Federation of Labour had, until the strains of 1967, increasingly become the strategist for its constituents since the merger twelve years before. And on the Continent where religion and politics and even centralized wage bargaining have helped the federations to a stronger position *vis-à-vis* their constituents, it is becoming respectable not only for members of competing federations to undertake joint action at workshop levels, but for federation officials to discuss trade-union unity amongst themselves. Everywhere trade unions have responded to wage and labour policies with a centralization of their own.

One result has been a professionalization of both the federations and their constituent unions and a tightening of organization all round – a development in line with the subtle, interrupted but unmistakable shift in the unions' public emphasis from confronting society on behalf of their members to confronting their members on behalf of society, from demanding 'more' to elaborating the difficulties in getting it. Inevitably, a further result has been to increase the distance between members and officials.

This distance is immense as it is. Seen through the eyes of union officialdom, the membership is a work-piece not an object for too great an identification. A study of British trade-

1. Frank Cousins, General Secretary, Transport and General Workers' Union, to the TUC, 7 September 1966.

union officers found that only a tenth of those who took other, known jobs after serving their unions were back on the 'shop-floor'; more than half became civil servants or officials in state corporations; and more than a tenth took managerial posts in private industry. It concluded that 'most full-time officers rate themselves amongst the holders of middle-class posts'.[2] Seen through the eyes of the membership, the gap is if possible even wider. Participation in branch-based elections is low, exemplified in Britain by the engineers' ten per cent average poll. Branch attendance is lower: mostly between four and seven per cent;[3] and the life of branch-based organizations – District Committees, Trades Councils and so on – is drained of content.

This is not due to centralization alone. The union branch – the old friendly society – has also lost out to the state (and even to the firm) as a welfare agent. It has been hit by workers' increased mobility, occupationally between jobs and unions, and geographically through the increased distance between home and work; as well as by the discordance of bread-and-butter issues which these bring into the branch. Most important of all it has been eclipsed in many places by workplace organizations more attuned to the members' current requirements. However, even without these factors, centralization and professionalism were bound to have shifted the unions' centre of gravity upwards.

Decentralization

Despite its own concentration, business has not on the whole responded to the trade unions' centripetal tendencies with centralized bargaining. On the contrary, it has tended to meet the uneven incidence of labour scarcity by negotiating variable local supplements to centrally bargained basic rates and conditions. Naturally only the biggest of firms are able to do so with any flexibility, by adapting production to local labour

2. H. A. Clegg, A. J. Killick and Rex Adams, *Trade Union Officers*, Basil Blackwell, 1961, pp. 85, 90.

3. B. C. Roberts, *Trade Union Government and Administration in Great Britain*, London, London School of Economics, 1956, p. 95.

conditions, or by siting new plants in areas of relative labour plenty (as in the drive south during and since the war in the US, the more recent '*saupoudrage*', or sprinkling, of the French electronics and chemical industries, or the subsidy-induced trickle northwards in British motors and engineering). But flexibly or not, most firms have found a need to couch their response in terms of the single plant.

Their method of payment enhances this localism. Most industrial workers are covered by one or other form of payment-by-results. In Britain this includes some three fifths of workers in large plants. In many cases the original rationale has disappeared with the shift from human- to machine-pacing of work speeds: yet PBR remains to provide a method of increasing wages that is both more flexible than any other and one less likely to spread from plant to plant. It constitutes the core of local bargaining and the greatest single pull away from centralized high-level negotiations.

Increasing size has had a similar effect. The firms with the greatest impact on the labour market are those best able to pass on increased costs. Because of this, and because in addition they have the resources to take a long view, they are able to go beyond single *ad hoc* wage rises under pressure to systematic wage increases foreseen and costed for years in advance – the 'improvement factors' which are being written into long-term wage agreements with increasing frequency. Since these firms also diversify more – and more easily – than most, they tend to act as independent spheres for wage bargaining and so add to its fragmentation. It has been estimated that something like half of all trade unionists in Britain are covered in this way.[4]

Add to these the increasing speed of innovation and the resulting variety of pay structures and service conditions; add too the incentive provided for each management to control internal 'drift' by systematizing bargaining *within* the firm – and the spontaneous drive towards decentralized, low-level negotiations can be seen to be fairly powerful.

4. John Hughes, 'British Trade Unionism in the Sixties', *Socialist Register 1966*, pp. 94, 111.

Managements attempt to keep such negotiations local wherever possible, by dealing with lay representatives of their own work-force rather than with national union officials. They do so, primarily because the local man has an 'intimate knowledge of the circumstances', but also because he is more likely to keep the issue within the plant, decide quickly and informally, and exercise greater influence on the members.[5] Some firms go as far as to formalize their intra-mural bargaining in 'Factory Negotiating Procedures'; and almost all provide opportunities for workshop representatives to act as bargaining agents. Bargaining at this level naturally results in sanctions being applied at this level, as will be seen more fully in the course of this chapter. And this in turn makes it all the more necessary to keep negotiations from shifting elsewhere.

Official policy often works towards the same outcome. The trend in wages policies is to narrow the scope of direct awards by lowering the level at which bargains are struck, while simultaneously trying to stop them spreading through comparison. In Britain, the Prices and Incomes Board has repeatedly advocated that bargaining *criteria* be settled centrally, while their *content* be decided on locally, even to the extent of tying wages to productivity on the railways.[6] In Holland, rigid adherence to central wage negotiations was abandoned in practice in 1958–9 when big employers were permitted to negotiate separately. Germany and Sweden have had similar experience.

The upshot is that some aspects of official wages policies together with unofficial practice pull towards localism, while the politics of labour policies in general and the search for consensus pull in the opposite direction – towards centralization and absorption of labour's institutions into society and the state.

Trade-union Reform

Trade unions have done their best to straddle the growing

5. Clegg, Killick and Adams, op. cit., p. 175.
6. National Board for Prices and Incomes, *Pay and Conditions of Service of British Railways Staff*, Cmnd 2873, HMSO, 1966, p. 26.

divergence. As can be seen in Chapter 5, they have accepted responsibility for large areas of national policy. They have also made some move, if only as a token, towards decentralized wage negotiations. In Britain a number of them are adopting the split-level bargaining pioneered in cotton textiles, where rapid technical change since the war persuaded the unions to back their comprehensive industry agreements with formal local bargains. In Germany, member unions have shaken themselves fairly free of the DGB's central wage policy since the mid-fifties; and IG Metall, largest of all, was reported early in 1966, not for the first time, to be 'seeking a complete overhaul of wage bargaining methods ... [whereby] much of the actual job evaluation and rate fixing would continue to be undertaken at the workplace, but within a framework and according to rules set by industry-wide agreements'.[7] In Holland this sort of flexibility was introduced at the end of the fifties; while since 1956, the major trade-union federation in Italy has increasingly 'decentralized its objectives' in recognition of the growing diversity in conditions in different firms and sectors.[8]

It is not difficult to envisage a system of decentralized bargaining – American unions have been running them since their formation. The real problems lie in enforcement; how to muzzle the workplace committees (taken up below); and how to define and police areas of operation so that one union – not twenty-two – would organize a single car plant in Britain, or better still, one – not scores – would organize a single industry like engineering. Associated are the need to replace geographical with workplace branches as the primary unit of organization, and to professionalize union administration.

While some progress has been made – in Britain, where the scene is most chaotic, there have been a few amalgamations in printing, building and shipbuilding; something has been done to streamline the administration of some of the larger unions; and 'there is far more willingness to discuss structural change,

7. Turner and Zoetewij, op. cit., p. 165.

8. Michel Bosquet, 'Aspects of Italian Communism', *Socialist Register 1964*, pp. 86–7.

and more flexibility, now' than as little as ten years ago [9] – the difficulties remain daunting. Unions have different policies and methods of work. Union officers naturally wish to retain their posts and their influence, and are not in practice subject to control by a membership that would disregard these things; 'rich union' officers resent having to pool resources with 'poor' ones, since, to take an example from Germany, 'the status within the DGB of the individual unions is not determined by the "degree of organization", but by the number of its members and its financial strength'.[10]

Sustaining these are marked differences in scales of contributions and benefit, and – above all – the fact that unions tend to support their claims by reference to traditional differentials, stressing the distinctions rather than the similarities between jobs. As the TUC General Council reported in both of its first two major reviews of trade union structure (1927 and 1944), the most intractable single obstacle in the way of closer collaboration and merger was 'the fear of loss of trade identity and autonomy'. The position has not changed since. Reviewing the findings of yet another TUC inquiry, George Woodcock, its General Secretary and himself a reformer, told Congress: 'We have come firmly to the conclusion that diversity of structure is a characteristic of British trade unionism and always will be.' [11]

Workplace Committees: Origins and Scope

A measure of the unions' failure to annex the emerging areas of bargaining has been the growth of semi-autonomous workplace organizations, like shop-stewards' committees, joint site committees, or whatever the local term used. In Britain they are made up of trade-union lay representatives, elected normally by a 'show of hands' and nearly always automatically accredited by their unions. In multi-union plants they tend to

9. Hughes, loc. cit., p. 109.

10. H. Gückelhorn, *Höhere Löhne, Wohltat oder Plage?*, 1958, p. 58.

11. Quoted by J. E. Mortimer, 'The Structure of the Trade Union Movement', *Socialist Register 1964*, p. 182.

include representatives from all unions. Partly because union rules governing representatives' activities are typically vague and rudimentary, sometimes non-existent; partly because of the growing diversity of production techniques; partly because of the workers' need to blur their own organizational demarcations when bargaining with management; and partly because of management's need for a recognizable local bargaining agent, these committees enjoy a large measure of autonomy.

They are also spreading fast. As engineering shop-stewards' committees, they first achieved prominence during and immediately after the First World War when they led a fight for the forty-hour week. Beaten back during the years of high unemployment, they re-emerged stronger during the Second World War, and have not looked back since. Today they number anything between 100,000 and 250,000 members – or more – nobody really knows;[12] they cover something like half the number of trade unionists in the country, typically in the largest establishments,[13] and they are spreading at a rapidly increasing rate both in traditional spheres and in new ones. In engineering, their original mass base, their number was increasing twice to three times as fast as membership in the late fifties and early sixties.[14] More significant is their encroachment on new industries: in 1966 alone, the system spread officially to building, to the docks, and to merchant shipping; and the TUC proposed for the first time in the seven or so decades of their existence, that stewards be fully integrated into the structure of industrial relations and of the unions.[15]

The committees have grown not only in number, but in strength. Throughout the West there has been a massive shift from the long, strategic, official and centrally directed strike typical of the earlier part of this century to today's short, local,

12. The lower limit – from A. I. Marsh and E. E. Coker, 'Shop Steward Organization in the Engineering Industry', *British Journal of Industrial Relations*, June 1963, p. 189; the upper – from *Trade Unionism*, evidence of the TUC to the Royal Commission, p. 145.

13. Cliff and Barker, op. cit., p. 87.

14. Marsh and Coker, loc. cit., Table I, p. 177.

15. *Trade Unionism*, op. cit., paras 406–18, pp. 141–5.

tactical and largely unofficial action.[16] In Britain, taking the period from the end of the Second World War, the number of strikes recorded by the Ministry of Labour has gone up from an average of 1,700 a year in 1946–50 to 2,700 a year in 1962–6 and the number of workers involved from 463,000 to over a million, while the number of days lost per worker has gone down from 4·2 a year to 2·9.[17] Since the number of reported strikes is a fraction of the total – as few as one twentieth in many cases [18] – and, given the trend towards shorter strikes, an ever-decreasing fraction; and since all but a minute proportion are 'unofficial', the influence of their typical organizers and leaders – the workplace committees – can be seen to be overwhelming.

The archaic system of bargaining and the chaotic trade-union structure in Britain have helped to bring workplace representation into prominence. But they are not fundamental to its existence. For even where 'inter-union diversity and structural gaps' in the British sense are absent or nearly so, workplace representatives operate and combine in a manner immediately recognizable here.

In Germany where industrial unions hold the field amongst manual workers, there is more than one claimant for the representative function. The *Betriebsrat* (works council) is provided for in law; its composition and functions – these are defined fairly widely – likewise. Associated with it in practice, particularly in large plants, are *Vertrauensmänner* (stewards) who act occasionally as the councilmen's eyes and ears amongst the workers, occasionally as a workers' pressure group on the councilmen, but normally in both capacities. *Vertrauensmänner* have no legal standing, none of the protection against dismissal and transfer that councilmen have, yet are usually able to meet and move in working hours and fulfil representative functions. In most large plants there are also trade-union representatives, narrowly conceived, also called *Vertrauens-*

16. See Arthur M. Ross and Paul T. Hartman, *Changing Patterns of Industrial Conflict*, John Wiley & Sons, 1960, Chapter 3.

17. *Ministry of Labour Gazette.*

18. See Cliff and Barker, op. cit., p. 82.

männer, who constitute a union cell in the plant, recruit for the
union and are enjoined to work closely with union councilmen.
Usually – not always – both *Vertrauensman* roles are filled by
the same people; occasionally councilmen double as stewards.
Sometimes, the three sets work in harmony; more often relations are strained by the part-absorption of councilmen in and
into management functions, so that 'management and the works
council often appear to the workers as complementary rather
than competing institutions'.[19]

The precise location of the representative function is obviously more ambiguous, diffuse and mobile in German industry
than in Britain; the authority of workplace committees is more
likely to be challenged; the unions are also better organized to
control their members at the workplace. Yet the same tendencies towards workplace autonomy and power are apparent in
both; wage drive added more than a third to centrally negotiated wage-rates in manufacturing and construction between
1950 and 1961;[20] trade unions are forced to adjust to firm-by-
firm bargaining. The results also sound very British: 'the
unions ... have completely lost contact with workshop realities:
communication between the top and members is insufficient;
and the two-way flow of information dries up in the middle
levels' of the union hierarchy.[21]

In France, workshop representation is even more important.
Provided for in law and working amongst a largely non-union
labour force, the 'enterprise committees' and workers' delegates
both keep the unions alive amongst workers and 'lead – quite
independently of the trade-union machine – the conflict with
the employer'.[22] In Holland, workshop committees led the

19. Otto Kirchheimer, 'West German Trade Unions: Their Domestic
and Foreign Policies', in Hans Speier and W. Phillips Davison (eds.),
West German Leaderships and Foreign Policy, Row, Peterson & Co.,
Evanston, Ill., 1957, p. 163.

20. Adolf Sturmthal, *Workers' Councils*, Harvard University Press,
1964, p. 201.

21. L. von Friedeberg, 'Betriebsräte und Vertrauensleute sollen sich
ergänzen', *Arbeitshefte*, Jg. 3, Nr. 4, 31 July 1964, p. 13.

22. Pierre Belleville, 'Die gegenwärtige Lage und die Probleme der
französischen Gewerkshaftsbewegung', *Arbeitshefte*, 1 July 1963, p. 27.

major revolt against wages control and the union leadership in the late fifties and sixties. In Italy, the ' "internal commissions" ... are but weakly controlled by the national unions'.[23] In the US, loose on-the-job committees have been making the running for both employers and union leaders increasingly since the early sixties.[24] Everywhere, whatever the union structure or system of bargaining, some form of democratic workplace representation exits.

It is not surprising. No union can conceivably do the work of such a committee. It cannot act as quickly; or act with such unconcern for repercussions elsewhere. It cannot have the same ready access to members and managements, nor sound opinion or formulate policy so soon after issues arise. In multi-union plants it could find taking any action at all almost impossible. Above all, there is always a 'basic conflict between the common shopfloor view in an active works branch or chapel, which sees itself as a "self-governing association within the workshop", and the formal rule-book position, under which the primary unit of union organization is invariably regarded as "but a minor and subordinate part of the trade union" '.[25] And if this is true of the most democratic and committed unions, it is infinitely more true of the vast majority which are neither and which, in addition, are so rapidly being drawn into formulating and prosecuting official labour policies.

Workplace Committees: The Drive to Control

Little is settled once a wage is agreed. The duration of work, its intensity, the conditions under which it is to be done (manning scales, hiring and firing, overtime, shift work, piece-rates, safety), are all subject to different interpretations in which the worker selling his ability to work and the management buying its source of profits are bound to contradict each other. When

23. Turner and Zoetewij, op. cit., p. 139.

24. See Stanley Weir, *A New Era of Labour Revolt, On the Job vs Official Unions*, Independent Socialist Club, 1966.

25. W. E. J. McCarthy, *The Role of Shop Stewards in British Industrial Relations*, Royal Commission on Trade Unions and Employers' Associations, Research Papers I, HMSO, 1966, p. 50.

conditions are in their favour workers attempt to exert some control in these spheres; when they are not, business tries to reassert its 'management prerogatives'. Wherever the initiative at any moment, a struggle for control goes on; and wherever that happens, the workplace committee is at its centre.

The shift in the locus of bargaining since the war has clearly enlarged the committees' role. In Britain, even the Ministry of Labour's imperfect data show a remarkable shift from strikes for more pay to strikes about 'wage-questions *other than* demands for increases', and – particularly – about 'working arrangements, rules and discipline'. In greater detail, an increasing proportion – three quarters of the total in 1960 compared with one third twenty years before – have centred on three main types of demand: that the intensity of labour be negotiated in the same way as wages; that changes in working arrangements, methods and the use of labour be similarly brought into the area of bargaining; and that workers be treated as people by managers and supervisors, not as 'hands' (these are the 'status' disputes).[26] A TUC inquiry into 'Disputes and Workshop Representation' confirmed that the majority of strikes involve issues of managerial authority;[27] while common sense suggests that many of the 'money strikes' are such for tactical or propagandistic purposes when their real content might justify a different description.

Strikes are only one weapon. Others – go-slows, working to rule, invoking formal procedure, relaxing discipline and so on – have been used with similar intensity.[28] Behind the details lies a simple fact: workplace committees will challenge mana-

26. H. A. Turner, *The Trend of Strikes*, Leeds University Press, 1963, p. 18.

27. *TUC Report 1960*, pp. 125–6.

28. The constitutional use of procedure, the easiest and best documented in Britain, can be used as an index. Amongst the engineers who account for two thirds of all disputes raised in this way the number of formal works conferences – the threshold for official union intervention – rose nearly four times as fast as the number of stoppages between 1956 and 1961, and union officials have been made to run to keep up with the business; their load of Works and Local Conferences doubled between 1955 and 1957 and has been increasing steadily since despite the boom in

gerial control wherever and whenever possible – directly if needs be, through their unions if convenient; on monetary issues if these are easiest, increasingly on others as their worker constituents question management's 'right' to regulate life at the place of work. And they will do so using the supreme argument of local organization – comparison, within the workplace and outside. For purposes of the challenge, every particular, every singularity of the workplace is fastened on as a negotiating counter and a source of added power. Most important are the piece-rates, incentive- or bonus-schemes tailored to each productive process. But beyond these there stretches a jungle of special payments and allowances – the 'dirt money', the 'heat money', the 'height money', the 'wet money' of cartoon industrial relations as well as lodging allowances, split shift allowances, clothing allowances and so on; and the even more tangled jungles of job evaluations and descriptions, overtime and shift-work arrangements, disciplinary issues, distribution of work loads, promotion, hiring and firing, introduction of new machinery and much else. Each is an occasion for testing the frontiers of control. Each marks off one committee from another.

In the event, the committees have made significant advances since the war. In many cases, they now exercise some control at least over all or most of the bargaining issues just mentioned; their convenors or chief stewards often enjoy direct and free access to works managers without the need to proceed through subordinate ranks. Normally, this has come about informally, for 'sometimes particular concessions are only possible on the tacit understanding that they would not be quoted either outside the firm, or even to other managers within the firm'.[29] But informally or not, the committees have done something to subordinate factory life to their constituents' wills.

informal conferences designed to avoid just that. (See Marsh and Coker, loc. cit., p. 183; A. I. Marsh and R. S. Jones, 'Engineering Procedures and Central Conference at York in 1959: A Factual Analysis', *The British Journal of Industrial Relations*, July 1964; A. I. Marsh, *Industrial Relations in Engineering*, Pergamon Press, 1965, p. 129n.)

29. W. E. J. McCarthy, op. cit., p. 28.

Workplace Committees: Horizons

Workplace committees are not unmindful of their role as representatives and organizers of labour power in every sense of the phrase. Half of those questioned in the survey already cited saw their primary function as the furtherance of workers' power: twenty-one per cent saw it in terms of '100 per cent organization', fourteen per cent as 'creating unity between workers', ten per cent as the 'fullest use by the rank-and-file of the democratic procedures of the union' and another five per cent as creating political consciousness.[30] Yet typically they see power in fairly narrow terms – in those of the shop or the plant.

In a way this is inevitable. They are, after all, *workplace* representative committees, separated from others by technical diversity, rapid technological change, the immensity of individual capital units and much else. Their function lies in interpreting the very specific wishes of their constituents; their power, in the confidence of those particular constituents; and their area of negotiation, in the conditions of production and methods of payment peculiar to each workplace. Since neither committees nor managements wish to relinquish their claim to a particular bit of territory, the marches between them are seldom, if ever, delineated in general terms; but are marked by concrete reference points, records of particular clashes. There is little in the shop-stewards' world that is abstract or general.

Nonetheless the committees do stretch beyond the individual workplace. Combine committees linking individual shop stewards' committees are to be found at some time or another in most multi-plant engineering firms in Britain; they have led a sporadic existence in building, linking large sites, on the docks, in shipping. Usually they arise in response to a particular crisis and then subside; sometimes they are broken by the very crisis that brings them into being – as in the British motor industry, summer 1966. Overall they seem to be growing in numbers and prestige, together with the scale of the business which defines their scope.[31]

30. Clegg, Killick and Adams, op. cit., Table 66, p. 262.
31. S. W. Lerner and J. Bescoby, 'Shop Steward Combine Committees in the British Engineering Industry', *British Journal of Industrial Rela-*

There have also been – less frequently and less effectively – industry-wide combine committees, notably in the motor industry, but also in shipping, the docks and electricity supply. These have been if anything less permanent, more a creature of particular crises and even weaker. For it is at this level where different local conditions and traditions need to be welded together in a common, general set of demands that the workplace committees lose much of their active support; and it is at this level that they challenge the trade-union machines head on.

This combination of strength in the workplace and weakness in transcending it lies behind the shifting pattern of extreme confrontations between individual managements and committees in the last decade or so in Britain. In different industries and at different times, isolated groups of workers have crowded managerial control so effectively that the conduct of business was jeopardized. These areas then became the scene for wider confrontations in which the firm as a whole, the industry, the state and, normally, the unions, bore down on the relatively isolated workplace organization and drove it back. This has happened repeatedly in the motor industry and the docks; it has happened at London Airport and amongst London busmen, amongst the seamen, electricity supply workers, printers and in a host of engineering factories. In each case, the rank-and-file organization carried its thrust towards control beyond management's sticking point and was rolled back. That in each case this was done more or less easily is a reflection of the narrow scope and relative isolation of most workplace organizations.

Their narrowness has another, closely related aspect. Dealing almost exclusively with bread-and-butter issues that can be decided in the workplace, they tend to ignore most of what goes on outside – whether the bus service to and from work or government economic policy. Far from leading to a heightened political commitment on the shopfloor, the spread of workplace representation has been accompanied by a decline in the industrial influence of all the traditional political parties. The Labour Party's retirement from the workplace has been mentioned (as has that of some workers' parties abroad).[32] The Conservatives, never strong, met their Waterloo in the mid-fifties with the collapse of the 'Monckton Era'. The Communist Party, still the most influential industrially, has suffered enormous damage over the last decade: having lost control over the electricians' and firemen's unions, and influence in the engineers' and miners', its presence within the trade-union machines is now small, attached to individuals many of whom reject party guidance, and some of whom are in active opposition. More important, its grass-roots support in industry is both declining and losing direction: there are fewer Communist Party industrial branches than five years ago, and none at all in the new, expanding industries like petrochemicals, plastics or synthetic fibres; and its most active worker-members in the older strongholds – engineering, building – are increasingly forced to look beyond the party and its sphere of influence when taking any initiative.

Part of the decline is undoubtedly due to the direction of the parties' policies – the Labour Party's escape from class to nation, the Conservatives' sustained attack on workplace organizations, or the Communist Party's drive for respectability. These leave little room for independent initiatives by workers as such. But the direction itself reflects a more deep-seated rejection of traditional politics by the workplace committees and their simultaneous annexation of the time, energy and interest of the most active workers.

Politics are not altogether ruled out. In the narrowest, technical sense, the steward's role is one of 'political adjustment', of satisfying his constituents without driving management to all-out, irresistible attack. In the wider sense too, workshop committees have played a crucial political role, as they did in Britain during and after the First World War,[33] or in Germany in the same period and particularly during the Revolution of

32. See above, pp. 119–20.
33. See Branko Pribićević, *The Shop Stewards' Movement and Workers' Control*, Basil Blackwell, 1959.

1918 [34] (or again in Hungary in 1956) [35] when the loss of room for compromise, of give, at the local workplace level transformed their narrow and fragmented concern with trade-union issues into a general political involvement. On those occasions the economics were stretched tight by war and its aftermath; and governments united with employers in resisting concessions.

The alchemy is as potent as it ever was; and while it would be ludicrous to think that the western economies are now under anything like the strain they bore during the First World War, room for local concessions is narrowing: official labour policies are everywhere invading the workplace, foreclosing on management's manoeuvrability, limiting the area of free bargaining at the local level, displacing the locus of decision-taking towards the centres of the national economy. The reasons – not the least being the committees' own success – have been reviewed and need no repeating. The results are fairly plain: the special features of each workplace become less important as even the strongest local organization weakens in its ability to exploit them; the pressure to coalesce and concert activity grows; and so does the pressure to conceive this activity in political terms, however rudimentary.

How far the committees evolve spontaneously towards seeking political solutions to trade-union problems is not very important in practice. Once out of the workshop, they inevitably come into contact with political organizations whose business it is to link fragmentary actions and particular demands into movements and programmes. As inevitably they became dependent to some extent on a political network, and their commitment to politics becomes fairly assured.

It is still early days for much evidence on these lines to have accumulated, although a little has – at least in Britain. In 1966 a handful of Workers' Solidarity or Defence Committees were

34. See Peter von Oertzen, *Betriebsträte in der Novemberrevolution*, Droste Verlag, Düsseldorf, 1963.

35. See Balázs Nagy, *La Formation du Conseil Central Ouvrier de Budapest en 1956*, Institut Imre Nagy de Sciences Politiques, Brussels, 1961.

formed, each covering different trades and different forms of
trade-union and political organization. Each arose out of a
particular dispute and received its initial impetus from the
workers directly involved casting about for support. Each
quickly attracted a nucleus of politically committed people;
and in each take-off from the particular circumstances of its
birth depended almost entirely on the political activists – not
all of them industrial workers – who were involved. In the
event, the political binding proved not strong enough. The
committees weakened within a few months; and have all but
dissolved. But they have shown a method and a direction which
could have immense consequences. Their inclusiveness makes
them, potentially at any rate, a powerful force, and their use of
industrial power for political ends, a revolutionary one. Given
the right circumstances such bodies could become an authentic
alternative to the established leadership.

Leadership

Relations between workplace committees and trade unions are
complex. They compete for the members' allegiance in many
ways and on many levels; at the same time they depend on each
other to fulfil their functions.

At the workshop level, the cards are stacked in favour of the
committees. Where they exist, they cover the entire workforce.
Few trade unions do. The committees are spreading fast, the
unions, caught between well-organized but declining traditional
industries and relatively unorganized expanding ones, are fairly
static, at relatively low 'penetration ratios'.[36] And although
unions are increasingly attracted to 'union shop' agreements
and a 'check-off' system of paying dues at source, this is an
arrangement to extend their *formal* authority. By itself it does
little to increase the real density of their coverage or the intensity of members' allegiance. By reducing their contact with
them, it might well have an opposite effect.

It is here in the matter of loyalty that the committees score
most. Stewards' constituencies are small – thirty to forty

36. See above, p. 89.

workers each in Britain.[37] They are chosen openly, are under the constant scrutiny of their electors, can be replaced without ceremony – a show of hands is often enough – and fairly easily. While in practice stewarding is a tried first step in managerial promotion, stewards are normally not driven by the cruder sorts of short-term ambition, or by any expectation of immediate personal gain.[38] Since they also collect eighty to ninety per cent of union dues both where this is provided for by Rule and where it is clearly contrary to Rule;[39] since they enrol almost all new members; act as the major channel for disseminating and interpreting union policy, to the extent of some seventy per cent of the flow of information to members,[40] and process most union claims at the initial, domestic stage; and since, most important of all, they get results and earn both respect and enmity from management for doing so, it is not surprising that they represent not only their union to most members but trade unionism itself.

Contrast this with the official machine. Its personnel is old, more than eight years older than the average steward, is more often appointed than elected, and forms a race apart in the way already described.[41] It encloses its members with the thinnest of thin films, perhaps one in 900 members in Britain overall. Union officers are inhibited by responsibilities that stretch beyond the single shop or plant; their jobs are not related to their effectiveness: their bread and butter comes from their members' difficulties yet their advice often stems from those of the 'nation'. At the ground-floor level of union life they are simply not in the race for members' loyalty.

Yet even here the committees are not in total command. Leaving aside periods of induced unemployment and insecurity

37. TUC, *Trade Unionism*, p. 45.

38. One fifth of a representative sample lost some money through being stewards while as a group they spent nearly as much of their own time on their representative functions as their firms'. Clegg, Killick and Adams, op. cit., pp. 154, 166.

39. McCarthy, op. cit., p. 39. Figures are for the AEU and NUGMWU respectively.

40. Gallup Poll figures for 1959, cited ibid., p. 40.

41. See above, pp. 124–5.

during which their base is liable to crumble in the general scramble for personal safety, they owe at least some of their authority to their union credentials, and some of the closeness with which they cover their constituencies to the variety of tasks they perform for and in the name of their unions. They rely on the union machinery in many of their lesser moves against management, as when using 'procedure'; are weakened or strengthened in major strike confrontations by whether they achieve official union recognition or not. In most cases their unions are the greatest single channel of communication with other fragments of the industrial world and so a source of support even during unofficial disputes. At a different level, the unions consolidate the gains they make and so act as a ratchet for more.[42]

Rivalry between the two is tempered by this mutual dependence. Neither is in a position to offer a total challenge to the other. The committees, in any case, are too fragmented to sustain a coherent, agreed view of the union machinery. When they oppose their own authority to that of the unions they do so sporadically, on particular issues, without casting themselves as a broad-spectrum alternative.

The unions' attitude, necessarily more explicit, is also more complex. For most, workplace representatives are a relatively new phenomenon, not yet absorbed into the formal structure. As late as 1956, two thirds of a sample of 134 British trade unions made no mention of them in their Rules, and of those that did, only six made provision for electing pure 'shop representatives', as against thirty-eight that provided for elections of joint shop representative and collector and forty-eight that provided for collectors only.[43] Where they do make provision, they reveal an almost universal unsureness of touch; methods of election are left vague, functions remain undefined, the process of formulating workplace policy is hazy, relations with other unions' representatives unspecified and so on. Yet in practical recognition of their importance, most large unions publish a *Shop Stewards' Handbook* or some equivalent and

42. See above, pp. 69–70.
43. B. C. Roberts, op. cit., p. 65.

in most of these some acknowledgement of their crucial role is to be found. Approval might be defensive in tone – 'it is very few who misuse their office', in the words of a TUC Report – but it is approval, and fairly general in the official machinery.

Attitudes change sharply as soon as the primary committees reach out to form links with each other. The effect of 'organizations linking a number of joint committees, either from several factories under the same ownership (e.g. BMC) or throughout an industry (e.g. electricity ... generating) is often a challenge to established union arrangements'. Even worse are the 'attempts to form a national centre or to call national conferences of stewards irrespective of the industry in which they work'. Here, warned the TUC, 'the aim ... is to usurp the policy-making functions of unions or federations of unions'; and it advised its affiliates 'to inform their members that participation in such bodies is contrary to the obligations of union membership ... to be more vigilant, and if, after a warning, a steward repeats actions which are contrary to rules or agreements, his credentials ... should be withdrawn'.[44]

Individual unions are hardly in a position to guard their authority so purposefully. Usually, officials realize 'that Combine members tend to be among unions' most active members' and are canny enough to turn a blind eye to their existence.[45] It is only when the activity of these 'most active members' seeks concrete expression that the unions act at all. But where they do, even the most tolerant, whatever their political slant, do so with surprising alacrity and considerable firmness, disciplining, suspending, expelling as they intone, 'unofficial bodies are not in the best interests of the industry'.[46] Normally however, they try to avoid open confrontation on these lines as being unlikely to produce lasting results. Willy-nilly even as they peck at it union officialdom finds itself nourishing the committee-

44. *TUC Report 1960*, pp. 129–30.

45. Lerner and Bescoby, loc. cit., p. 161.

46. Frank Foulkes, then Communist President of the electricians' union and Chairman of the Electricity Supply Industry National Joint Council. Quoted in Cliff and Barker, op. cit., p. 99, *q.v.* for other examples.

cuckoo. There is, after all, little else to feed. Increasingly, the tendency is to tame it, incorporate it; to displace rather than destroy it.

One method is to compete in terms of effectiveness. As the figures on page 70 show, the official machinery can move fairly fast when they feel it necessary to keep within sight of the committees. They can even eclipse them for a time. But while there is some evidence that unions in Britain are becoming a little more willing to declare strikes official,[47] they cannot travel too far down that particular road. They are too committed to national agreements to be free to compete in augmenting them locally, and too deeply involved in national economic policy to want to. Besides, there is always the possibility that they might succeed in domesticating the committees: after all twenty-nine per cent of the stewards asked did say they would like to become a paid union official as against only five per cent who would refuse because they wished 'to remain in the rank-and-file'.[48]

In Britain, where the committees are strongest organizationally, domestication takes a number of forms. One is ideological. In 1962 the TUC agreed with the British Employers' Confederation to promote shop-steward training, and to press unions to agree their syllabuses with management in exchange for releasing stewards from work with pay. 'Outside the factory,' went one critical reaction at the time, 'in the kinds of courses now proposed [the stewards] will be taught to consider problems in the terms and concepts of an alien class.'[49] The agreement was followed by a tightening-up of trade-union education and its centralization in TUC hands.

Another is organizational. Unions are becoming increasingly disenchanted with piece-rate systems as being the greatest single support to the committees' autonomy; and they are also swinging round to supporting the 'union shop'. Some – the electricians and engineers, for example – have gone, or are about to

47. See, for example, Marsh and Jones, loc. cit.
48. Clegg, Killick and Adams, op. cit., pp. 170, 171.
49. *International Socialism* 13, Summer 1963, editorial on 'Shop Stewards', p. 4.

go, very far indeed in professionalizing the major functions of stewards.

It is perfectly possible for unions to incorporate the workplace committees if they wish to. Some have already done so, in Britain. It has been done abroad. But there are limits to what they can accomplish in this way. In most countries there is a felt need for workplace unity which both transcends union divisions and covers gaps left in union organization. In all, even where organization is based on factory branches, there is a basic conflict between the branch's subordination to union – and ultimately, national – policy and the workers' drive to control factory life. Both require organization and if the workplace committees as we know them are prevented from providing it, they will tend to be displaced. As it is, recent developments in some Midlands car factories might turn out to be of uncommon significance:

> ... militant stewards – goes one report – have insisted that the convenors may not handle grievances by themselves, but only in association with the particular steward involved *and* at least one *ad hoc* representative of the men. In this way control over the bargaining process is kept at the shop-floor level wherever possible.[50]

Throughout western capitalism, workers now feel needs which their union machinery cannot hope to satisfy, least of all machinery increasingly mortgaged to official economic policy. Appeals to traditional loyalties can have little lasting effect – they are too confident, and their confidence too solidly based on skill, scarcity and the achieved results of their own widely dispersed actions. Yet if they are not involved in the aims of their unions and their twilight committees not integrated into the union machinery there can be no hope for the consensus on which wage and labour policies ultimately rest. And without such policies there can be little life in the fragile stability achieved since the war. For as the instabilities of the arms economy touched on in Chapter 3 develop and place

50. Colin Barker, *International Socialism* 27, 'Notebook', p. 4.

increasing strains on established society, and as that society responds with increasing centralization, the decline of the traditional restraints on workers' action might become crucial. For these are circumstances in which the fragments of direct reformist activity tend to fuse and in which mass reformism of this sort is liable to be suffused with revolutionary purpose.

Part 3   *Predictions*

8. The New Arms Race

The ABM decision

On 18 September 1967 the American Secretary of Defense announced that the United States would build 'a relatively light and reliable Chinese-oriented Anti-Ballistic Missile system'. It was a dramatic turnabout. As late as January he had told a Senate Committee: 'After studying the subject exhaustively, and after hearing the views of our principal military and civilian advisors, we have concluded that we should not initiate an ABM deployment at this time.' [1] Two months later he was still instructing a House Committee that the best counter to a Russian ABM system was more offensive missiles, not a competitive American ABM. [2]

The decision had been resisted for a long time, [3] and for good reasons; the systems were too complex to be expected to work, yet not complex enough in principle to cope with the tasks assigned them. They were required to perform with near-total reliability in an unprecedented, unsimulable environment, yet they were more liable to failure than most 'high risk' weapons systems, most of which had come nowhere near their target

1. Robert S. McNamara, Testimony to the Joint Session of the Senate Armed Services Committee and the Senate Subcommittee of the Department of Defense Appropriations, 23 January 1967, excerpted in *Bulletin of the Atomic Scientists*, June 1967.

2. 'I do not think there is a senior civilian or military officer in the Defense Department that does not believe that (1) we should react to the [Soviet] ABM deployment by expanding our offensive force, and (2) we have the technical capability to react in such a way as to assure our continued capability to penetrate that ABM defence. None of us are in any doubt about that.' (*Department of Defense Appropriations for 1968*, Hearings Before a Sub-Committee of the Committee on Appropriations, House of Representatives, quoted in Jeremy J. Stone, *The Case Against Missile Defences*, London, The Institute for Strategic Studies, Adelphi Paper No. 47, April 1968, p. 5.)

3. Presidential vetoes were placed on the Nike–Zeus system in 1959

specifications.[4] They were expected to respond to surprise attack with hair-trigger sensitivity and yet provide stiff-trigger assurance against accidental and unauthorized firing.[5] They were vulnerable to rapid obsolescence from related and unrelated advances in offensive weapons[6] and from constantly changing attack patterns.[7] They were amazingly expensive – $50 billion for a full system[8] and, which was more crucial, three or four times as costly as the improvements in offensive techniques that could overwhelm them.[9] Above all, they threatened to undermine the basis of East–West military stability – the balance of terror, or the power to assure each other's destruction in any circumstances, *regardless of who struck first*.[10]

(Eisenhower) and 1962 (Kennedy), and on Nike-X in 1963 (Kennedy) and 1966 (Johnson).

4. Only two out of eleven such systems met performance specifications between 1960 and 1967, another reached a 75 per cent standard, two more a 50 per cent standard, and the rest 25 per cent or less. (Richard A. Stubbing, 'Improving the Acquisition Process for High Risk Electronics Systems', Congressional Record, 7 February 1969, p. S 1450.)

5. See Herbert F. York, 'Military Technology and National Security', *Scientific American*, August 1969, p. 25.

6. Nike–Zeus and Nike-X were both rejected on these grounds before they could have been deployed. (See US Congress, Senate Committee on the Armed Services, *Military Procurement Authorization*, Fiscal year 1964; and US Congress, House Subcommittee of the Committee on Appropriations, *Department of Defense Appropriations for 1964*, Part I, pp. 434–5).

7. Some offence scenarios are set out in Richard L. Garwin and Hans A. Bethe, 'Anti-Ballistic Missile Systems', *Scientific American*, March 1968.

8. ibid.

9. Abram Chayes and Jerome B. Wiesner (eds.), *ABM, an Evaluation of the Decision to Deploy an Antiballistic Missile System*, New York, Evanston, and London: Harper & Row, 1969, p. 46; Lawrence W. Martin, *Ballistic Missile Defence and the Alliance*, The Atlantic Papers No. 1, Paris: The Atlantic Institute, 1969, pp. 14–15.

10. This balance had precise quantitative definition – an ability to cause 'more than 120 million immediate deaths, to which must be added deaths . . . by fire, fallout, disease and starvation' and to destroy 'more than 75 per cent of the productive capacity of each country' 'within a day and perhaps within an hour'. (Garwin and Bethe, loc. cit.) It sustained a

This balance has now been upset. Since the cheapest and most effective way to neutralize a missile defence is to overwhelm it, any ABM deployment, however feeble or rudimentary, or even any hint of such deployment, presents an irresistible argument to the other side to multiply hugely its strike force. It can do so by increasing its missile armoury as the Russians have been doing since 1966. More significantly, it can do it – as both sides are – by arming its missiles with Multiple Independently Targetable Re-entry Vehicle (MIRVs) and other devices to amplify their effect. This more than quadruples the number of warheads a missile can now deliver; in the future it promises to multiply them ten- or twelve-fold.

Such a quantum jump in offensive power must be matched. But parity in MIRVs is qualitatively different from parity in missiles; once the ratio of warheads per booster rocket becomes larger than the ratio of warheads per target, each side will, in theory, possess a margin of destructive power over and above what is needed to overwhelm the other's missiles. Add to that developments in anti-submarine warfare techniques which threaten to end the current invulnerability of underwater missile-carrying craft by 1972, and the attractions of a first-strike, pre-emptive strategy in offence and for a 'launch on warning' defensive counter become obvious. With them grows a cumulative, self-justifying pressure to raise offensive power by a truly prodigious multiple until such time as technological change will have reduced the ratio-gap to what it was many tens of billions of dollars previously.[11] Meanwhile all thought

special language, and even special kits, such as the widely advertised 'standard Nuclear Bomb Effects Computer Slide Rule'. It provided sufficient mutual security to the two super-powers for them to reach agreement on a number of issues: atmospheric testing (1963), proliferation (1968), the siting of nuclear weapons (1959, 1967 and 1969), and a lot else. And, it sustained a pause in the deployment of existing weapons and the introduction of new ones that lasted for most of the 1960s.

11. The size of the multiple can be gauged from the following testimony by Hans A. Bethe, former Member, President's Scientific Advisory Committee, and Nobel Prizewinner for Physics, 1967: 'If we deploy the Sentinel system we shall probably be tempted to improve it in quality and to increase the number of our anti-missiles so as to keep up with

of restraining proliferation will have collapsed in the turmoil of world-wide military and political uncertainty.

There are many 'ifs' and 'buts' here. A first-strike strategy can be operational only when MIRVs become more reliable and accurate than they are, ABMs more effective even against disjointed, post-strike attack, and anti-submarine techniques also vastly improved. Yet the slide towards it is irresistible, for once missile-defence gets within range of technical *feasibility*, as it did in the United States by the end of the fifties, imputing its *deployment* to the enemy is only a matter of time. By 1960 American military planners had endowed Russia's 'Tallinn' *air*-defence system – itself designed to anticipate an American bomber programme that never took off – with an anti-*missile* capability it was never intended to carry. More accurate, or less biased, intelligence came too late to reverse the US's react-ive plunge into perfecting the penetration aids that have culminated in MIRV. That plunge in its turn pushed Russia inexorably to missile defence ('Galosh', from the early sixties) and to a huge missile deployment and MIRVing programme (the SS-9s, late sixties). As inevitably Russia's moves pre-cipitated the US decision on ABM.

The logic is inescapable. At its most superficial, it is fuelled by mutual distrust; by common ignorance, and mutual trans-ference, of outside 'Chinese' intentions; and by conservative 'worst-case' contingency planning. At a deeper level it reflects the interests of a 'military–industrial complex' – the phrase is President Eisenhower's – which, in the US, creates one in nine jobs, generates one tenth of gross national product, involves 100,000 companies, allows massive cost overruns in military research and development assignments while exercising neglig-

---

the developing Chinese threat ... to a point where it would appear threatening to the Soviet Union ... we shall ... tend to deploy 3–5 times as many anti-missiles as are actually needed. The Soviets, seeing this, will in turn overestimate our building plans, as well as the capability of our ABM ... they will then build again 3–5 times as many ICBMs as are actually necessary to penetrate our defenses. In this manner a relatively minor Chinese buildup may easily lead to a Soviet buildup of ten times that number. This in turn will cause us to respond in kind with

ible budgetary control, provides outstanding profitability without clear reference to performance, and so on.[12] At an even deeper level it reflects – as is shown in Chapter 3 – the pitiless inertia of a world society organized for unrestrained competition at a stage in its development when competition converges on calamity.

It is not a negotiable logic. Whatever the Strategic Arms Limitation Talks might achieve in formalizing the coming round of arms escalation, they will be unable to annul it. Both sides have already made their commitments. Their power structures are set. And some of the consequences are already in train.

The most dramatic is the US decision to withdraw from Vietnam. It is not yet fulfilled, and every effort is being made to obscure it at home as well as to the shaky régimes of South East Asia. But once the 'Tet offensive' had forced the US to identify its priorities, had 'performed the curious service of fully revealing the doubters and dissenters to each other, as in a lightning flash', in the words of a minor participant,[13] there was no doubt about which way the decision would go.

---

an increase of our ICBM force.' ('The ABM, China and the Arms Race', based on testimony before the Disarmament Subcommittee of the Senate Foreign Relations Committee, 6 March 1969, *Science and Public Affairs*, Bulletin of the Atomic Scientists, May 1969, pp. 41–4).

12. See Adam Yarmolinsky, 'The Problem of Momentum', in Chayes and Wiesner (eds.), op. cit., pp. 144–9. The ABM system is in this lucrative tradition. In its early phase it promises to involve 15,000 firms in 72 Congressional districts in 42 states, to create a million jobs, and, in the words of a stockbroking firm, to 'shake the money tree for electronic companies' (ibid.). And this for all time. As Dr John S. Foster, Director of Defense Research and Engineering, put it to a Senate Committee: 'Because of the enormous quantities of equipment involved, and the near rapid rate at which the technology changes, to maintain an effective system one would essentially have to turn over the whole system, the whole $20 billion system, every few years.' (*US Armament and Disarmament Problems*, Hearings before the Subcommittee on Disarmament of the Committee on Foreign Relations, US Senate, 3 February to 3 March, 1967, p. 15).

13. Townsend Hoopes, then Under-Secretary of the Air Force, *Atlantic Monthly*, September 1969.

For the growing queue of military contractors, armed-forces strategists and Congressional lobbyists, impatient for the new weapons systems, Vietnam has a distraction from the essential American interest. Indeed, as President Nixon pointed out in his tour of the region (July 1969) the whole of South East Asia was a distraction. The war had become the enemy and the Pentagon by and large joined the flight of doves.

As early as January 1969 the Department of Defense was blocking escalation in the field by shifting $3·5 billion of its budgetary requests from Vietnam to expenditure on the new weapons. By the end of the year 60,000 GIs, one fifth of all American combat troops, had been withdrawn, many of them from two particularly sensitive areas in Quang Tri province and in the delta. Most significant of all, from early 1968 onwards news of peace in Vietnam brought out the bulls, not the bears, on Wall Street.

Another consequence has been middle-class America's sudden apprehensiveness at the potential danger and colossal waste wrapped inside the new military thinking. Last year (1969), for the first time in a generation, Congress forced the Pentagon to take a cut – $3 billion – in its already trimmed budget request. The Department of Defense had to fight unbelievably hard for Senate to approve – by one vote – the Safeguard ABM system for missile-site defence, itself a retreat, under considerable and well-organized pressure, from the earlier Sentinel system. It has since had to accept an outside investigation in order 'to restore public confidence' in itself (Laird). Not since the early days of World War II has the political monolithism of middle-class America looked so shaken.

These are merely a beginning. For if any one decision can be said to signal a new course in something as complex and embracing as the capitalist system, the ABM decision is such.

The Ghetto Revolt

One sphere in which the consequences are likely to be quickly felt is the blacks' battle for incorporation into contemporary America.

The blacks form the last of the great washes of unskilled workers into the urban economy. Some four million have migrated from the rural South since 1940. They are now more urbanized than the white population as a whole, and the largest single differentiated block of people in existing city areas. But they have come too late to be absorbed as they are into the American economy. The number of non-agricultural un-skilled jobs has dropped sharply as a proportion of the total since the war, and the number of central city jobs of this type has fallen absolutely. And although the number of black graduates has been growing, it is easier in almost every way to supply the needed skills from abroad than from the ghettos; as many as 30 per cent of labour-force immigrants are now classed as 'technical managerial and professional' compared with 6 per cent of employed blacks.[14]

The result is a pitiless redundancy of the ghetto population; unemployment double or more the rate for whites in every category, rising to between a quarter and a third of all black teenagers; underemployment eleven times the rate for whites;[15] a bunching of blacks at the bottom of the wage scale at three times the white concentration; a devaluation in black earnings compared with white, at all levels of skill, that cost the ghetto community $4·8 billion in 1966, or more than three times its loss from 'abnormal' unemployment,[16] and much more in the same vein. The result is also their near-total exclusion from an urban political structure that is wasting away as fast as its integrating functions decline: four years after the 1965 Voting

14. From Anthony Scott, 'Transatlantic and North American Inter-national Migration', paper read to the International Economic Associ-ation Conference on *Mutual Repercussions of North American and Western European Economic Policies*, Algarve, Portugal, 28 August–4 September, 1969 (roneo), pp. 10–11; and US Department of Labor statistics.

15. The underemployed are defined as part-time workers looking for full-time jobs, full-timers on under $3,000 a year, and unwilling drop-outs from the labour force. See *Report of the National Advisory Commission on Civil Disorders* (Riot Commission *Report*), New York, Bantam Books, 1968, p. 257.

16. ibid., pp. 254–5.

Rights Act opened elective office to them, black elected officials numbered 'well over 800' out of a total 520,000 or 0·153 per cent for 12 per cent of the population.[17]

Until challenged by a new urban generation – specifically by the 'life-long resident of the city ... somewhat better educated than the average inner-city Negro ... [but] working in a menial or low status job ... not full time' in the words of the Riot Commission's 'profile of a rioter' – this exclusion was as uncoordinated as it was unquestioned, a product of centuries of violent discrimination and discriminatory violence. But since then, particularly since the all-American flare-up of 1967 and 1968, there has had to be a national policy. And, although in theory this could be anything from penning the blacks in the increasing insufferable 'present policies', through relative enrichment of a separate existence, to full integration,[18] actual policy has plainly hardened around the first.

Within a year of the Riot Commission Report, Congress had expunged most of its freshly adopted conciliatory decisions; the Manpower Development and Training Act was frozen; the Job Corps cut; the Neighborhood Youth Corps pruned; legislation for open public employment, for 'cease and desist' orders in job discrimination aborted; public housing projects, public rent aid, urban denewal plans, model cities – all under the Housing Act of 1968 – were approved, only to have their funding slashed; and the 1968 Civil Rights Act, which was to have been lubricated with $11 billion, was left with $2 billion. Later Nixon helped to kill the Voting Rights Act and lined up the Federal Government behind Mississippi's attempt to postpone desegregation in schools.

The repressive apparatus has also hardened. Within the same year, four fifths of the army reserve – over 200,000 men – received 'training in civil disturbance'; local police unions were unusually active in forming national links and in cam-

17. *One Year Later, An Assessment of the Nation's Response to the Crisis Described by the National Advisory Commission on Civil Disorders*, Washington DC, Urban America Inc. and The Urban Coalition, 1969, p. 91.

18. Riot Commission *Report*, pp. 395–6.

paigning for freedom to indulge in the anti-black licence white opinion polls suggest they should have [19] and police authorities conspired to destroy the most militant black political groupings.

The dangers are obvious. As repression toughens and its apparatus unwinds itself from constraint, it becomes less discriminating and its impact wider. Techniques and attitudes formed on both sides in ghetto fighting are transferred to campuses, where they help fuse components of protest into a self-sustaining, largely colour-blind revolutionary culture. They invade the army, where, aided by the strains of enforced intimacy and the revulsion from war in Vietnam, they have already resulted in boycotts of riot duties, in posting refusals, in mutiny and in on-camp race riots. However, more important than all in the long run is their spread into organized industry.

Compressed into the hardest and nastiest trades, blacks now constitute a disproportionate share of the manual work force in many of the basic, organized sectors of production and distribution – from 28 per cent in water transportation services to 12 per cent in the manufacture of motor cars and other transportation equipment, through construction (16·4 per cent), mass transit (16·2 per cent), steel and other metal products (15·6 per cent), food (15 per cent), and so on.[20] Despite widespread and active discrimination, they are solidly represented in many of the unions that cover these trades – 12 per cent of the membership in non-building international unions.[21] In some areas their predominance is greater. In New York, for example, they form a majority or near it in public transport, sanitation, garment-making, postal and welfare services; and a substantial minority in private transport, railways, the docks, distribution and local government.

In such trades and areas they are doubly squeezed – as blacks

19. See *One Year Later*, pp. 68, 81–2.
20. From Equal Employment Opportunity Commission, *Equal Employment Opportunity Report No. 1*, Washington D C, Government Printing Office, 1968, Table, pp. A1–A4. Figures relate to 1966.
21. Equal Opportunity Employment Commission, *Local Union Report EEO–3*, Press release, 1969. Figures relate to 1967.

and as workers; and have tended increasingly to take the lead in unofficial industrial struggles, often through 'black caucuses', and almost always with some support from white fellow workers. Support has not always been easy to get in the teeth of racist provocation by boss and union alike, but once gained it has usually fed on the clubbing and gassing it has met at the hands of authority.

It need hardly be said that America's ruling racist culture is not going to dissolve at the first flash of worker – or student – solidarity, nor at the early signs of strain in the armed forces. Until now these have in any case been no more than primitive, localized responses to passing pressures. At most, they have been a fervent wish on the revolutionary fringe. Yet one thing is plain: the United States dares not exclude its 22 million blacks any more than it can fully incorporate them. It might try both, but every move increases the probability of colour-blind joint action on the job; and each such action enlarges the scope for a revolutionary attack on American society.

The consequences of ABM are bound to sharpen the dilemma. As it is, the arms industries use more skilled – and therefore less black – labour than the general run of American industry; 16 compared with 13 per cent in the broad professional group, 21 compared with 13 in the skilled manual grades, and 24 compared with 19 per cent in semi-skilled grades.[22] As they increase their technological bias the arms industries will be able to do even less to relieve the press of black workers around unskilled jobs and will make even more anguished the slip in the black escalator to skilled ones.

The shift affects economic management as well. No American administration can avoid trying to douse the inflationary pressures that increased military expenditure and the attendant skill shortage will create throughout the economy. The consequences in the ghettos could well be appalling. As it is, the mild restraints of last Summer pushed up general unemployment to 4 per cent by September. That meant a rate of about 8 per cent unemployment for blacks, 10 per cent for blacks in

22. Max A. Rutzick, 'Worker Skills in Current Defense Employment', *Monthly Labor Review*, September 1967, pp. 17–20.

'poverty neighbourhoods' and nearly 40 per cent for black teenagers. And that, in turn, probably means a long and very violent Summer preceding the mid-term elections of 1970, when aspiring Congressmen will be outbidding each other in vote-getting proposals for ghetto overkill. And that again can only add to the steady rise in violence and to the hardening of responses throughout American society, at a most crucial time – when an unusual number of labour contracts come up for renewal after a long period of substantial price increases. Nor is the economic groundswell the end of the story. The black has already been made a scapegoat for middle-class America's general apprehensiveness at the ABM strategy. As *The Times* pointed out,

the Administration sided with Mississippi [on school desegregation] so as to ensure Senate approval of its Sentinel [sic] anti-ballistic missile programme. Senator John Stennis, of Mississippi, is the chairman of the armed services committee. Without his help the programme would have been defeated.[23]

There is more to come. Faced with the enormousness of the expenditure, and given that the ABM lends substance to a Fortress America concept, with all that that implies in political narrow-mindedness and reaction, the search for scapegoats can easily become a hunt. With it will grow, no doubt, a realization in the ghettos that survival lies in organization and in transmitting the shock-waves of repression as directly as possible down the seismic fault of American capitalism – the conflict between labour and capital.

National Revivals and Regional Strains

The ABM decision is not a purely American, or even a Russo-American, affair. European capitalism cannot hope to escape the consequences. Whichever way it now turns – whether to renewing the interrupted progress towards economic and political regroupment, or to competitive national attachment to the United States – one thing is plain: the new arms race will give

23. 24 October 1969.

a prodigious extra thrust to the polarization of military, economic and political power away from Europe, and result in a defensive concentration – and drain – of capital on the Continent, and a drain of resources away from it, such as have seldom been seen.

The problems are not new. To take their regional aspect only,[24] almost every European country has been forced in the last ten years or so to adopt or strengthen regional planning. In Britain, where slow overall growth, a high degree of industrial homogeneity and a fairly settled society combine to make regional concentration and drain a leisurely process, more than ever before is now being ploughed into job creation and new industrial building in the Development Areas.[25] In France the current Fifth Plan now ending contains unprecedented measures to divert new jobs to the ten western regions.[26] In Italy no less than one quarter of the South's income has been pumped in from outside since 1951.[27]

Yet there is not much to show for the effort. In Britain the number of new jobs generated in the Development Areas is less than the number of new jobless created in them, and only a quarter to two fifths of the number needed every year.[28] In France migration from the South and West (*le désert*

24. Concentration of capital need not mean physical concentration in some areas, and physical drain from others. It used to, and has left behind it, the filthy, airless, mobbed and shrieking industrial wastelands we live in, as well as their wasted and distraught rural surroundings. Even now, when concentration need not be – and is not always – unpremeditated and unplanned, regional hypertrophy and atrophy are its normal accompaniment.

25. See Gavin McCrone, *Regional Policy in Britain*, London, Allen & Unwin, 1969, pp. 198, 271.

26. Geoffrey Denton, Murray Forsyth and Malcolm MacLennan, *Economic Planning and Policies in Britain, France and Germany*, Allen & Unwin, 1968, p. 315.

27. Average for 1951–60. See Hollis B. Chenery, 'Development Policies for Southern Italy', reprinted from *The Quarterly Journal of Economics*, 1962, pp. 515–47, in Lionel Needleman (ed.), *Regional Analysis, Selected Readings*, Penguin Books, 1968, Table 3, pp. 204–5.

28. See A. J. Brown *et al.*, 'Regional Problems and Regional Policy', *National Institute Economic Review*, November 1968, p. 51.

français) to the Paris region was expected to fall by no more than one third despite the special provisions.[29] In Italy the rip-tide goes on – it has brought two million people to the North in two decades, has shattered urban services and administration and, if the despairing Mayor of Milan is to be believed, can be absorbed only at sixteen times the current level of 'social expenditure'.[30] Elsewhere in Europe, from Scandinavia to Spain, the same is true. Nothing seems able to pin down capital or stem its drain towards the bursting industrial congestions. As crude raw materials become less important, and as transport cheapens and becomes more flexible, industry becomes more footloose; and as its size grows with it its dependence on large markets, big concentrations of labour and skill, and big government, so do the attractions of Megalopolis-Europe (the quadrilateral linking Birmingham, Paris, Frankfurt and Amsterdam).

And since Megalopolis-Europe straddles six independent states, no one of them dares or can impose its will, particularly on super-mobile American business. Penalties drive it over the border as de Gaulle found during his most anti-American phase,[31] while subsidies are quickly matched and, after the intra-European accounts are settled, become another drain of European resources to the United States. Even public capital cannot be saddled with responsibility for regional policy for all time. Ultimately its performance is measured in the same terms of competitive efficiency as is that of private investment. So concentration goes on, and with it the drain of jobs, skills, raw labour, youth and intelligence from the periphery of the system.

The costs in human and social terms are immeasurable – not least because there are no valid yardsticks for such things in our society. But even in recognized terms, they are high and could become damaging. Unemployed and under-used resources in the drained areas are pure loss when economic

29. See Denton *et al.*, loc. cit.
30. Speech reported in the *Financial Times*, 10 September 1969.
31. See Jean-Jacques Servan-Schreiber, *The American Challenge*, Penguin Books, 1969, p. 28.

growth of whole countries becomes a normal mode of competition.[32] There are costs in migration: every new recruit to the high-wage boom areas adds another twist to the inflationary spiral and hastens the point at which growth needs to be choked off.[33] There is the electoral threat to parties in power.[34] But above all, concentration and drain pose a threat to the integrity of the national state.

This is not a new threat. At the back of Whitehall's mind as it gingerly picks a way through the minefield of Northern Ireland lurks a history of revolt, suppression and ultimate with-

32. 'An essential condition for the fulfilment of the Plan', ran the Introduction to the British Labour Government's ill-fated *National Plan*, 'is the fullest use of manpower in the less prosperous regions of the country.' (*The National Plan*, p. 11).

33. See Lionel Needleman, 'What Are We To Do About the Regional Problem?', *Lloyds Bank Review*, January 1965, pp. 46–7; and Needleman (ed.), op. cit., pp. 14–15.

34. In Britain a strong case can be made for seeing the major parties' futures in terms of a regional protest vote; as strong as the case for seeing their regional policies in terms of electoral insurance: the problem-region vote was first felt acutely in 1959, when Scotland swung 1·4 per cent *against* the Tory government of the day compared with an average opposite swing of 1·2 per cent in Great Britain as a whole (Butler and Rose, op. cit., p. 205). Government spending in the Development Areas then rose quickly from £8·6 million in 1958–9 to £51 million in 1960–61 (McCrone, op. cit., pp. 114, 145). It then fell off – by half the following year, and by another third the year after that – only to double in 1963–4 (ibid., p. 145) during the run-up to the 1964 elections – which the Tories lost. With Labour balanced precariously in power, expenditure on job creation was stepped up, but not enough to bring in the regional vote. In 1966 the swing towards Labour in Scotland, Wales and the Severn constituencies was less than two thirds the otherwise exceptionally uniform national average (Butler and King, 1966, pp. 261–2) and the straight nationalist vote in Scotland took a big stride forward (ibid., p. 290). Since then nationalism in Scotland and Wales has become an electoral force at both Parliamentary and local levels.

In France, although de Gaulle was broken by the mass strike of May–June 1968 and the capital flight that followed, what finally brought him down was the rejection – by referendum – of his regional policy. And in Italy, despite its conservatism – or rather because of it – the Communist party is able to lean more and more heavily against the doors to Parliamentary power, because these doors have been so thoroughly battered by the regional tornado.

drawal south of the border, so damaging to the British state as to make a repetition north of it unthinkable.

Yet repetition is not ruled out. Despite the large and growing public subsidy to the Stormont régime since the end of the Second World War,[35] Northern Ireland has normally run a large, positive trade surplus with Britain.[36] Since the figures on which this conclusion is based are *net*, arrived at *after* the public transfers have had their offsetting effect, there is a strong presumption that the private drain *towards* Britain is now perhaps double the public transfer in the reverse direction. The figures are imperfect[37] and the logic far from watertight.[38] But if they mean what they appear to mean, they have serious political implications. For with the drain of capital go a drain of jobs (40,000 down between 1949 and 1964)[39] and a drain of

35. Some £45 million a year in the early sixties; rather more than that after the Civil Rights rebellion at their end. (From R. J. Lawrence, *The Government of Northern Ireland, Public Finance and Public Services 1921–1964*, Oxford, Clarendon Press, 1965, p. 73; and press reports.)

36. Exports averaged some £28 million a year more than imports (8·8 per cent) for twelve years, rising to a peak of £45 million in 1967, the last year for which figures are available. (From Government of Northern Ireland, Economic Section, *Digest of Statistics*, No. 31, March 1969, Belfast, H M S O, table 103, p. 68.)

37. Cf. Lawrence, op. cit., p. 49: '. . . throughout the province's whole history, financial questions of great public interest and importance were shrouded in secrecy'.

38. A consistent export surplus such as Northern Ireland's with Britain could arise from payment for services based on Britain, such as shipping, insurance, banking and so on – but it would be hard to justify its size and particularly its rapid recent growth in this way. The surplus could also reflect a British investors' habit of supplying the components of new fixed capital in the Six Counties not from Britain but from the rest of the world, with which Northern Ireland runs a consistent trade deficit – but there seems no obvious reason for this to have happened in any but a minor way. Or it could mean that a high proportion of Northern Ireland's exports to the rest of the world are trans-shipped in British ports but recorded as exports to Britain, and that an opposite, unrecorded trans-shipment of imports via British ports, does not occur. As in the other cases, this might happen, but there seems no reason to suppose it does consistently or on a large scale.

39. Government of Northern Ireland, *Economic Development in Northern Ireland, Including the Report of the Economic Consultant*

people (131,000 to Britain, 1951–66).[40] With it go also the unemployment (nearly four times the level in England), underemployment ('activity rates' 85 per cent the level in England),
poverty (incomes two third the United Kingdom average),
slums – and open defiance.

At root, this is a working-class defiance. The Northern Irish
middle class is neither of a mind nor in a position to protest too
loudly. Its protestant majority owes its very being to policing
the drain – and incidentally to excluding, brutally and with
verkramptelik consistency, the Catholic minority from any part
of such duties. While that small minority, for its part, has never
wanted more than a share of these duties under Orange flag or
Green. But for the working class, particularly the Catholic
working class, the situation is very different. For them to tackle
almost any immediate problem – as workers, as Catholics or as
Irishmen – is to confront the realities of drain and its social
organization, and to be impelled towards a far-reaching solution – the expropriation of British capital, whether in Northern
or in a reunited Ireland.

It is not an easy solution to propagate, let alone achieve. It
formed nonetheless the hidden core of the appeals to *all*
workers in Northern Ireland, irrespective of creed, that went
out from Radios Free Derry and Free Belfast in the late
summer of last year. It forms, very explicitly, the central theme
of the revolutionary left that has emerged from behind the
barricades and is now seeking to expand its influence across the
Border southwards.

For reasons peculiar to Britain and Ireland, the concentration and drain scouring western capitalism have evoked the
strongest response in the Six Counties. But it is only a matter
of degree. In almost every country – from Quebec in Canada
to Wallonia in Belgium, from Scotland in Britain to Vizcaya in
Spain – dormant and dead nationalisms, regional and linguistic
movements are clambering out of the vortex, demanding the

Professor Thomas Wilson, Belfast, HMSO, Cmd 479, 1965, pp. 23, 31,
33.
40. McCrone, op. cit., p. 20.

impossible from capitalism – an even distribution of wealth and power. Many are plaintive enough – lower-middle-class representations for placement in lower-bureaucratic niches. Some are obscured – as in Italy, Autumn 1969 – by the violence of the ingestion into growth areas. But in all there is a revolutionary current that reads the effects from the system, and that is waiting to flow outwards along the fractures which show during any period of general dislocation.

The Student Movement

The number of students in the West has grown four or five times faster than population since the war. They now form a huge, unstable mass, over ten millions strong in North America and Western Europe, more conscious of itself and its particular situation than any other.

Their growth in numbers has been in response to capital's prodigious and growing appetite for technical and social-manipulative skills.[41] It has been an uncoordinated and explosive growth that has wrenched most of the established patterns in higher education out of shape. Facilities built for a few dozens are made to serve hundreds and thousands.[42] Teacher–student relationships cast in a personal, democratic mould are twisted into the up–down contacts of an exercise yard. Above all, the social and ideological functions of higher education have been bent. Its institutions, designed as semi-autonomous seminaries for society's high-priests, where an intellectual élite was separated out from its social peers, encouraged to

41. In the words of the Robbins Report, '. . . progress – and particularly maintenance of a competitive position – depends to a much greater extent than ever before on the skills demanding special training'; and, they went on, 'there is a function that is much more difficult to describe concisely, but that is nonetheless fundamental: the transmission of a common culture and common standards of citizenship. . . . This function, important at all times, is perhaps especially important in an age that has set for itself the ideal of equality of opportunity' (Committee on Higher Education, *Report*, London, H M S O Cmnd 2154, 1963, pp. 6, 7).

42. There are some 500 seats in the University of Paris library – for 156,000 students. The Sorbonne tries to accommodate 30,000 students in a building reconstructed (1901) for 1,700.

know itself and to evolve into creative exponents and critics of the ruling ideology, have been compelled to double as training establishments for society's clerks, where instrumental skills are learned and where their underlying values are buried or embalmed.

One result has been a sharp deterioration in the norms of behaviour in Senior Common Rooms as colleagues factionalize and fight for 'eternal values' or 'market realities', 'autonomy' or 'government grants', 'excellence' or 'democracy' in a fantasy of tangled purposes. Another, closely related, is the environment of incoherence and spite presented to the mass of students. But a more important result by far is that an increasing number of students are herded into close proximity to the future men of power while being themselves excluded from future influence; and is provided with tokens of achievement only to find them steadily devalued by the spread of higher education.

Naturally they are frustrated, resentful and rebellious. Naturally the minority destined for better things is no less resentful of being forced to conform to herd logistics, even if temporarily. Neither can remain unaffected by being crowded inside a social decompression chamber in which the controls have plainly jammed and in which moreover they are exposed to never-ending ideological stimulation and choice.

Bruised expectations feed rebellion. They do not cause it. What does is the mental rough-handling which students, particularly social-science students, undergo in being conscripted for ideological service. Socially isolated but physically concentrated, subjected to ritualized punishment and reward, and, in the actual teaching, to incantation, rationalization and subterfuge, students undergo a harsh and complex conditioning which has few parallels outside the campus.

Not many can resist. Most become resigned to their futures, many of these after severe emotional and psychic disturbance.[43]

43. During their undergraduate lives, 1–2 per cent of students can expect to experience 'severe psychiatric illness of a type requiring hospital admission'; another 10–20 per cent will 'present ... an emotional or psychological problem sufficient to need some treatment'; and a further

Some drop out. But the minority who do resist discover they can do so only by founding their opposition on solid ideological and political grounds. In the authentic tones of student militancy, 'the unrest of sociology students cannot be understood unless one questions the social function of sociology [44] or,

the source of the alienation of the student of social sciences [lies in a] ... training [which] consists in learning at best how to tinker with the machine called society, at worst in the mastery of an esoteric jargon which, it is alleged, explains the world [but which] does no such thing.[45]

That ideas and their social function are the substance of campus confrontations is significant. It means that militant students are easily able to identify their *sectional* concerns,

---

20 per cent 'will report transient psychological or even psychosomatic symptoms ... [including] many of the well known pre-examination stress reactions'. These figures probably understate the incidence of strain, since they are derived from 'cases presenting to clinical services', not from surveys.

While it is 'impossible to say whether these rates for students are different from the rates in the age-group as a whole, because ... comparable opportunities to record such rates are lacking' off-campus, it is significant 'that psychiatric illness is more common in art students than in science students'. (Anthony Ryle, *Student Casualties*, Allen Lane, The Penguin Press, 1969, pp. 35–8.)

44. Daniel Cohn-Bendit, Jean-Pierre Duteuil, Bertrand Gérard, Bernard Granautier, *Why Sociologists?*, leaflet circulated on the Nanterre campus, mid-March 1968, reproduced in Alexander Cockburn and Robin Blackburn (eds.), *Student Power*, Penguin Books, 1969, pp. 373–8.

In context, 'the practice of organizing capitalism creates a mass of contradictions; and for each particular case a sociologist is put to work. ... Each seeks an explanation of his partial problem and elaborates a "theory" proposing solutions to the limited conflict that he studies. Thus while serving as a "watchdog", our sociologists will make his contribution at the same time to the "mosaic" of sociological "theories" ... the unrest of sociology students cannot be understood unless one questions the social function of sociology ... the sociologists have chosen their camp – that of business managements and of the state. ... In these conditions, what does the "defence of sociology" ... really mean?'

45. Chris Harman, Dave Clark, Andrew Sayers, Richard Kuper, Martin Shaw, *Education, Capitalism and the Student Revolt*, London, International Socialism, n.d. [1969].

such as are connected with their particular physical and social location, with the *general* social interest; or, in traditional terms, they can identify their own *trade-union* matters with the *political* concerns of society at large. It also means that every sectional confrontation in the world off-campus, from wage demands to Vietnam moratoria, can sound an immediate echo on-campus where it takes political form *ab initio*. Given the abstract nature of the principles that unite – and divide – them, it means too that students can fairly easily overcome distance, language and custom to form into large, even international, movements; and given the fact that student time is more or less unstructured, particularly in the sensitive ideological subjects, it means that they can act most effectively as mobile link-men in industrial struggles, racial battles, general political campaigns, or whatever.

That they *can* do all this is not to say they always *do* it. Abstractions and universals lead as easily to indiscipline, romanticism, sectarianism, intellectual thuggery and sudden alterations in mood as to deep understanding and involvement. But if and when they do act beyond the campus, they can become important, as has been shown in more than one place in the sixties, and nowhere with such *éclat* as in Paris, May–June 1968.

Even before the ABM decision it proved impossible to prevent the growing student mass from going critical from time to time. After it, particularly as its frightening irrationality unfolds and the social and political consequences become apparent, it will become increasingly difficult to prevent the student mass from reacting permanently.

The Revolutionary Prospect

It is one thing to suggest that the ABM decision might rupture the localized pressure points in western capitalism. It is another altogether to say that the system has therefore entered a stage of general collapse. For that to happen, the shock of the decision would have to run through the deepest rift of them all – the conflict between labour and capital.

There is a lesson to be learned from France. Ten years before the insurrectionary strikes of May–June 1968, the country was bogged down in an expensive, unwinnable war in Algeria. It was torn by war-induced conflict at home. The Treaty of Rome had just been signed, and French capital looked as if it was about to lose much of its protected home market to its European partners.

Change was clearly necessary, and de Gaulle the man to introduce it. Algeria was abandoned. The armed forces were converted from a conscripted para-police force to a professional modern military one with a high technology bias. Gross investment was stepped up by more than a third to 26 per cent of GNP in ten years, and an orgy of business concentration took place.[46] Most spectacular of all, French capital climbed rapidly into one of the strongest financial positions in the west as its reserves in gold rose from virtually nothing to $5 billion in five years and still went on growing. The Gaullist policy of *tous azimuts* appeared to be paying off, economically as well as militarily.

Somebody had to finance it. Partly it was France's Common Market partners that did so – Germany in particular.[47] But the really big bills were paid by the French workers. Two devaluations (1957 and 1958) and several austerity programmes ensured that labour costs in France rose less than in any other Common Market country up to 1966, and were lower than that in all bar Italy.[48] Although output grew faster than in all of Western Europe, again with the partial exception of Italy, faster than in

46. See above p. 38.

47. De Gaulle's protectionist policy in Africa came to rest substantially on German credits to the common Development Fund. By the end of his Presidency, French agriculture was drawing nearly one billion dollars a year out of the Common Agricultural Fund, most of it on German account. The same was true in many of the other areas of Community financing.

48. Wages and social-insurance costs between 1959 and 1966 averaged 43·5 per cent of market price in France, compared with 48·8 per cent in the Netherlands, 47·2 per cent in Belgium, 47·1 per cent in Germany, and 42·8 per cent in Italy (*Le Monde*, Weekly Selection, 17 September 1969).

the U S, twice as fast as in Britain, real wages lagged [49] – by 1966, French industrial workers were the second-worst paid in the Common Market, and working the longest hours.[50] They were also paying the highest taxes.[51]

By then they had had enough. That year there were 2½ million strike-days compared with a million the year before. 4·2 million followed in 1967. The régime responded with deflation, unemployment and violence. The big bang of 1968 was in the making. When it came, workers who had been asking for *more* and had been denied, reached out for *control* – and were quickly offered *more*. Abandoned by *le parti de la trouille* (the party of funk), as de Gaulle called the Communists, and almost completely innocent of an alternative, revolutionary, leadership, they took it.[52]

The material results were immediate and impressive. Wages jumped by 14 per cent in a few months – 9–10 per cent in real terms; unemployment virtually disappeared; the working week began to slide from 45–8 hours to 40; trade unions were recognized in diehard firms like Citroën, and application for union membership rose by a third.

The political demonstration was even more impressive. The

49. Between April 1964 and April 1968, real wages in France rose 12 per cent compared with 19 per cent in the Netherlands, 17 per cent in Belgium, 15 per cent in Italy, 14 per cent in Germany.

50. Average industrial wages in France were the equivalent of $0·83 an hour for a 47·3-hour week, compared with $1·21 in Luxemburg, $1·15 in Germany for a 43·9-hour week, $1·00 in Belgium, $0·95 in the Netherlands and $0·67 in Italy, but for a 37-hour week.

51. At $467 per head, more than twice the Italian figure, France led the European league; consumer taxes provided 58 per cent of tax revenue compared with 45 per cent in Germany and 39 per cent in the Netherlands.

52. Most writing in English on the French upheaval of 1968 concentrates on what was most accessible emotionally and geographically to foreign intellectuals – the student insurgency. This is true of even the best accounts, like Patrick Seale and Maureen McConville's (*French Revolution 1968*, Penguin, in association with William Heinemann, 1968). A more balanced view can be found, however, amongst the revolutionary *groupuscules*, as in Tony Cliff & Ian Birchall, *France, the Struggle Goes On*, London, Socialist Review Publishing Co. Ltd, 1968.

big bang breathed life into just about every tenet of revolutionary faith in the West. It showed the power of workers in revolt; the amplification revolutionary ideas achieve when they are; the importance of revolutionary leadership, even of the amateur, inchoate and short-winded student variety; and the decisive role a professionally organized revolutionary party could play in coordinating, politicizing and replenishing a mass upheaval of that amplitude.

The antecedents and longer-term results are as significant, if less dramatic. They show that the need to compete in an increasingly integrated market compelled French capital to load unacceptable burdens on its workers, and that when it came to the crunch, it could still find the resources, with US and German help, to remove them. Helped by labour's lack of political preparedness, and the low price-tag it therefore put on *control*, French capital was able to buy it off with material benefits.

There is nothing to show that the pressures on the smaller national capitals are about to relax, or that they can respond in any other way. Allowing for a change of scene to Italy, perhaps, or, more probably, to Germany, the contrary would appear to be true even without the additional pressures generated by the new arms race.

As it is, conditions for European capital have deteriorated sharply in the two years since. American firms have lodged deeper in the most advanced sectors of industry, wresting control from French nucleonics, and strengthening their hold on the new electronics- and solid-state-physics-based industries. American raids on European financial resources have grown in frequency and become more damaging.[53] And the US dollar has emerged strengthened from the European financial

53. US firms cornered over 60 per cent of all European bond issues in 1968, doubling short-term interest rates throughout the area to a phenomenal 12·5 per cent in a matter of nine months to mid-1969; and came very close to wrecking orderly management in domestic capital markets. (See Margaret L. Greene, 'Growth and Retrenchment in the Euro-Bond Market', *Federal Reserve Bank of New York Monthly Review*, August 1969).

challenge and the speculative crises of 1967–9; gold is all but demonetized, major European currencies have been forced into unwanted adjustment, and the western world now holds three fifths of its official reserves, or four fifths of reserves including Euro-dollars, in American currency.

At the same time, European capital's own attempt at protective regroupment is faltering as each country piles control on control in an effort to head off the financial stampedes that have punctuated the growing internationalization (or dollarization) of their economies. They cannot hope to succeed: the problems they are trying to cope with have themselves created the huge, volatile, increasingly mobile mass of Euro-dollars, which has broken through all international monetary dykes in the last three years and which, moreover, is uncontrollable in principle.[54] But they can try. And in doing so each jacks up its idle reserves relative to GNP and to trade by running an export surplus and by raising domestic interest rates to keep or attract foreign funds. Each is then edged into the fundamental Gaullist paradox of dispensing wage restraint, enforced mobility of labour, legislative controls and deflation while pressing for greater effort from its already highly employed workers. And since discretionary economic management has failed so miserably in coping with a growing, more integrated and therefore more complex world, and since this failure has occasioned a general retreat from the politically responsive Keynesian tradition to an earlier one of inflexible rules and contractual obligations,[55] the paradox brings the system as such, not merely its agents into focus.

Some of the results have already shaken Europe. A West-wide wage explosion followed the French strike and added

54. Euro-dollars amounted to some $40 billion, or more than world gold reserves, at the end of 1969. They are essentially bank-money, a *private* recognition of obligation, created like any bank deposit with one crucial difference – they are generated abroad, beyond the reach of their owner's state and law.

55. In the words of Professor Milton Friedman, the new mouthpiece for old orthodoxy: '. . . we simply do not know enough to be able to use either fiscal policy or monetary policy as a flexible and sensitive instrument to control the course of the economy'.

something like a twelfth to average earnings in the region. In Italy millions of workers registered half a billion strike days in 1969, including three general strikes which here and there boiled over into insurrectionary confrontations on a wider front – not only for pay, hours, better conditions and control over their unions, but, in the South, for jobs, and in the North for the housing, services and welfare which only Government, that is politics, can provide. In France similar upheavals, spiced moreover with extremist memories, have been contained only at enormous, unrepeatable cost to French capital, as employment hit its ceiling, wages and prices rose, and reserves continued to drain away and the trade deficit to grow throughout the year despite devaluation.

But it was in Germany that the most significant, if undramatic, action took place. For it is in Germany that workers have both made most material gains and lost relatively most in the last twenty years.[56] In a huge chain-reaction of strikes, some official but mostly unofficial, that preceded the General Election of last September, workers in all the major industries won pay increases between 10 and 15 per cent. It was an exhilarating experience, unlikely to be forgotton.

It is also unlikely to be repeated quickly and easily. For German capital has been forced to up-value its currency and absorb a big rise in wage costs. It has been propelled by the French collapse to take on almost single-handed the European *Gleichschaltung* against the US. It is being pushed by America's ABM-inspired retreat into neo-isolationism to emerge as a military power in its own right. In a word, even German capital, the mightiest in Europe, has entered the Gaullist trap. Unable to assume the continued quiescence of its

56. Wage incomes rose $3\frac{1}{2}$ times in current values between 1950 and 1967, and 'entrepreneurial and self-employed' (including farm-) incomes five times. In the same period average wage incomes fell from five sixths of the latter to just over half; and the workers' share of private wealth from two fifths to under one quarter. Meanwhile, Germany in the sixties has been one of the few countries in the world in which public expenditure on 'social objectives' has lagged behind the growth of output; and to this day its outlay on education is the lowest in the Common Market relative to GNP and only half the proportion spent in Britain.

working class, yet unable any longer to give in easily to its demands, it is lining up a social explosion that has all the ingredients of France 1968, and more – for this time the sides will be armed with hindsight and political purpose.

Germany is not Europe, and Europe not western capitalism. But their problems are similar. Scale for scale the costs and results of maintaining competitiveness in an increasingly un-stable economic environment are no greater for German – or European – capitalism than are the costs and results for the US of maintaining military power in an ABM world. As we have seen, the costs are likely to be prodigious. The results could be even more so. For western capitalism is once again creating conditions for the convergence of working-class protest and revolutionary politics that could change the world. Whether or not that convergence will take place in the seventies depends as much on the revolutionaries as on anything discussed here.

Alphabetical List of Major References

ABC of the TUC, London, Trades Union Congress, 1966.

Allen, Victor L.; *Trade Unions and the Government*, London, Longmans, 1960.

American Economic Review, Journal of the American Economic Association.

Arbeitshefte, Sozialwissenschaftliche Vereinigung Duisburg eV, Duisburg.

Atlantic Monthly.

Bagehot, Walter; *The English Constitution* (1867), with an Introduction by R. H. S. Crossman, London, Fontana Library, 1963.

Baran, Paul A., and Sweezy, Paul M.; *Monopoly Capital*, New York and London, Monthly Review Press, 1966; Penguin, 1968.

Basso, Lelio; 'The Italian Left', *Socialist Register 1966*.

Basso, Lelio; 'A New Socialist Party', *International Socialist Journal*, April 1964.

Basso, Lelio; 'Old Contradictions and New Problems', *International Socialist Journal*, July 1966.

Beckerman, W., and Associates; *The British Economy in 1975*, Cambridge University Press/National Institute of Economic and Social Research, 1965.

Belleville, Pierre; 'Die gegenwärtige Lage und die Probleme der französischen Gewerkschaftsbewegung', *Arbeitshefte*, 1 July 1963.

Bethe, Hans A.; 'The ABM, China and the Arms Race', *Science and Public Affairs*, May 1969.

Blondel, Jean; *Voters, Parties and Leaders*, Harmondsworth, Middlesex, Penguin, 1965.

Bortkiewicz, Ladislaus von; 'On the Correction of Marx's Fundamental Theoretical Construction in the Third Volume of Capital', in Sweezy (ed.), *Eugen von Böhm-Bawerk*, etc.

Bosquet, Michel; 'Aspects of Italian Communism', *Socialist Register 1964*.

Brady, Robert; *Crisis in Britain*, Cambridge University Press, 1950.

British Journal of Industrial Relations, London, London School of Economics.

Brown, A. J., *et. al.*; 'Regional Problems and Regional Policy', *National Institute Economic Review*, November 1968.

Bulletin of the Institute of Statistics, Oxford.

Burchardt, F. A.; 'Output and Employment Policy', *Bulletin of the Institute of Statistics*, Oxford, January 1942 (reprinted in UOIS, *Studies in War Economics*).

Butler, David E.; *The British General Election of 1951*, London, Macmillan, 1952.

Butler, David E., and King, Anthony; *The British General Election of 1964*, London, Macmillan; New York, St Martin's Press, 1965.

Butler, David E., and King, Anthony; *The British General Election of 1966*, London, Macmillan, 1966.

Butler, David E., and Rose, Richard; *The British General Election of 1959*, London, Macmillan, 1960.

Carter, C. F., and Williams, B. R.; *Investment in Innovation*, Oxford University Press, 1958.

Central Statistical Office; *Economic Trends*, London, HMSO; monthly.

Chaynes, Abram, and Weiser, Jerome B. (eds.); *ABM, an Evaluation of the Decision to Deploy an Antiballistic Missile System*, London, Harper & Row, 1969.

Chenery, Hollis B.; 'Development Policies for Southern Italy' [1962], in Needleman (ed.), *Regional Analysis, q.v.*

Clegg, H. A., Killick, A. J., and Adams, Rex; *Trade Union Officers*, Oxford, Basil Blackwell, 1961.

Cliff, T., and Barker, C.; *Incomes Policy, Legislation and Shop Stewards*, London, London Industrial Shop Stewards' Defence Committee, n.d. [1966].

Cliff, Tony, and Birchall, Ian; *France, the Struggle Goes On*, Socialist Review Publishing Co., 1968.

Cockburn, Alexander, and Blackburn, Robin (eds.); *Student Power*, Penguin Books, 1969.

Committee of Public Accounts; *Second Report 1966–1967*, London, HMSO, 1966 (HC 158).

Committee on Higher Education, (*Robbins*) *Report*, London, HMSO, 1963 (Cmnd 2154).

Committee on the Working of the Monetary System; *Report*, London, HMSO, 1959 (Cmnd 827).

Corina, John; 'Labour and Incomes Policy', *New Society*, 19 November 1964.

Crosland, C. A. R.; *The Future of Socialism*, London, Jonathan Cape, 1956.

Denton, Geoffrey; Forsyth, Murray; MacLennan, Malcolm; *Economic Planning and Policies in Britain, France and Germany*, London, Allen & Unwin, 1968.

Dow, J. C. R.; *The Management of the British Economy 1945–1960*, Cambridge University Press/National Institute of Economic and Social Research, 1964.

Dowse, Robert; 'Trade Union MPs in Opposition', *Trade Union Affairs*, Summer 1964.

Economic Trends; London, HMSO for the Central Statistical Office, monthly.

Economist, the; London, weekly.

Economist Intelligence Unit, The; *The Economic Effects of Disarmament*, London, EIU; Toronto, University of Toronto Press, 1963.

EEC, *The Development of a European Capital Market*, Report of a Group of Experts appointed by the EEC Commission, Brussels, 1966 (the Segré Report).

Equal Employment Opportunity Commission; *Equal Employment Opportunity Report No. 1*, Washington, DC, Government Printing Office, 1968.

——; *Local Union Report EEO–3*, 1969.

Fellner, William; *Competition Among the Few*, New York, Alfred A. Knopf, 1949.

Fellner, William; Gilbert, Milton; Hansen, Bent; Kahn, Richard; Lutz, Friedrich; de Wolff, Pieter; *The Problem of Rising Prices*, Paris, Organization for European Economic Cooperation, 1961.

Feuersenger, Marianne (ed.); *Gibt es noch ein Proletariat?*, Frankfurt/Main, Europäische Verlagsanstalt, 1962.

Foa, Vittorio; 'Incomes Policy: A Crucial Problem for the Unions', *International Socialist Journal*, June 1964.

Friedeberg, L. von; 'Betriebsräte und Vertrauensleute sollen sich ergänzen', *Arbeitshefte*, July 1964.

Gaitskell, Hugh; *Recent Development in British Socialist Thinking*, London, Cooperative Union, n.d. [1956].

Gaitskell, Hugh; *Socialism and Nationalization*, London, Fabian Society, 1955.

Galbraith, John Kenneth; *The Affluent Society* (1958), Harmonds-worth, Middlesex, Penguin, 1962.

Galbraith, John Kenneth; *American Capitalism, The Concept of Countervailing Power*, (1952), second revised edition, Harmonds-worth, Middlesex, Penguin, 1963.

Galbraith, John Kenneth; 'The New Industrial State', 1966 BBC Reith Lectures, *Listener*, 17 November – 22 December 1966.

Galbraith, John Kenneth; *The New Industrial State*, London, Hamish Hamilton, 1967; Harmondsworth, Middlesex, Penguin, 1969.

Garwin, Richard L., and Bethe, Hans A.; 'Anti-Ballistic Missile System', *Scientific American*, March 1968.

Gilbert, Milton; 'The Postwar Business Cycle in Western Europe', *American Economic Review*, May 1962 (Papers and Proceedings of the 74th Annual Meeting of the American Economic Associa-tion, New York, NY, 27–9 December 1961).

Goldthorpe, John H., and Lockwood, David; 'Affluence and the British Class Structure', *Sociological Review*, July 1963.

Government of Northern Ireland, Economic Section; *Digest of Statistics No. 31*, March 1969, Belfast, HMSO.

——; *Economic Development in Northern Ireland, Including the Report of the Economic Consultant Professor Thomas Wilson*, Belfast: HMSO, 1965 (Cmnd 479).

Greene, Margaret L.; 'Growth and Retrenchment in the Euro-Bond Market', *Federal Reserve Bank of New York Monthly Review*, August 1969.

Gückelhorn, H.; *Höhere Löhne, Wohltat oder Plage?*, Stuttgart, 1958.

Harman, Chris, Clark, Dave, Sayers, Andrew; Kuper, Richard, Shaw, Martin; *Education, Capitalism and the Student Revolt*, London: International Socialism, n.d. [1969].

Harris, Nigel; 'The Decline of Welfare', *International Socialism*, Winter 1961.

Harris, Ralph, and Seldon, Arthur; *Choice in Welfare 1965*, London, Institute of Economic Affairs Ltd, 1965.

Harrison, Martin; *Trade Unions and the Labour Party Since 1945*, London, George Allen & Unwin, 1960.

Hughes, John; 'British Trade Unionism in the Sixties', *Socialist Register 1966*.

International Financial News Service; Washington, DC, weekly.

International Labour Office; *The Cost of Social Security 1958–1960*, Geneva, 1964.

International Labour Office; *Labour Costs in European Industry*, Geneva, ILO Studies and Reports, New Series No. 52, 1959.

International Socialism; London, quarterly.

International Socialist Journal; Rome, bi-monthly.

Joint Trade Union Advisory Committee to the OECD, *Some Joint Trade Union Advisory Committee Comments on the Report of the Group of Experts on the Problem of Rising Prices*, reprinted in *Trade Union Affairs*, Autumn/Winter 1961.

Kirchheimer, Otto; 'West German Trade Unions: Their Domestic and Foreign Policies', in Hans Speier, and W. Phillips Davison (eds.), *West German Leaderships and Foreign Policy*, Evanston, Ill., Row, Peterson & Co., 1957.

Kuznets, Simon; *Postwar Economic Growth*, Cambridge, Mass., Harvard University Press, 1964.

Labour Party, *Annual Reports*.

Labour Party, *Industry and Society*, London, 1957.

Lawrence, R. J.; *The Government of Northern Ireland, Public Finance and Public Services 1921–1964*, Oxford University Press, 1965.

Le Monde, weekly selection, Paris.

Lerner, Shirley W., and Bescoby, John; 'Shop Steward Combine Committees in the British Engineering Industry', *British Journal of Industrial Relations*, July 1966.

Liebman, Marcel; 'The Crisis of Belgian Social Democracy', *Socialist Register 1966*.

Listener, the; London, weekly.

Lloyds Bank Review; London, quarterly.

McCarthy, W. E. J.; *The Role of Shop Stewards in British Industrial Relations*, Royal Commission on Trade Unions and Employers' Associations, Research Papers I, London, HMSO, 1966.

McCrone, Gavin; *Regional Policy in Britain*, London, Allen & Unwin, 1969.

Maddison, Angus; *Economic Growth in the West*, New York, The Twentieth Century Fund; London, George Allen & Unwin, 1964.

Maddison, Angus; 'How Fast Can Britain Grow?', *Lloyds Bank Review*, January 1966.

Marsh, A. I.; *Industrial Relations in Engineering*, Oxford, Pergamon Press, 1965.

Marsh, A. I., and Coker, E. E.; 'Shop Steward Organization in the Engineering Industry', *British Journal of Industrial Relations*, June 1963.

Marsh, A. I., and Jones, R. S.; 'Engineering Procedures and Central Conference at York in 1959: a Factual Analysis', *British Journal of Industrial Relations*, July 1964.

Martin, Lawrence W.; *Ballistic Missile Defence and the Alliance*, The Atlantic Papers No. 1, Paris, The Atlantic Institute, 1969.

Miliband, Ralph; *Parliamentary Socialism*, London, George Allen & Unwin, 1961; Merlin Press, 1964.

Milne, R. S., and Mackenzie, H. C.; *Marginal Seat, 1955, a study of voting behaviour in the constituency of Bristol North East in the general election of 1955*, London, Hansard Society for Parliamentary Government, 1958.

Ministry of Labour Gazette, London, monthly.

Monthly Labor Review, Washington, DC.

Mortimer, J. E.; 'The Structure of the Trade Union Movement', *Socialist Register 1964*.

Nagy, Balázs; *La Formation du Conseil Central Ouvrier de Budapest en 1956*, Brussels, Institut Imre Nagy de Sciences Politiques, 1961.

National Board for Prices and Incomes; *Pay and Conditions of Service of British Railways Staff*, London, HMSO, 1966 (Cmnd 2873).

National Bureau of Economic Research; *The Rate and Direction of Inventive Activity: Economic and Social Factors*. A conference of the Universities–National Bureau Committee for Economic Research and the Committee on Economic Growth of the Social Science Research Council, Princeton, NJ, Princeton University Press, 1962.

National Institute Economic Review; London, quarterly.

The National Plan; London, HMSO, 1965 (Cmnd 2764).

Needleman, Lionel (ed.); *Regional Analysis Selected Readings*, Harmondsworth, Middlesex: Penguin Books, 1968.

——; 'What are We to do about the Regional Problem?', *Lloyds Bank Review*, January 1965.

New Left Review; London, bi-monthly.

New Society; London, weekly.

Nicholson, R. J.; 'The Distribution of Personal Income', *Lloyds Bank Review*, January 1967.

OECD; *Capital Markets Study*, 4 volumes, Paris, 1967 and 1968.

OECD; *Government and Technical Innovation*, Paris, 1966.

OECD; *Policies for Price Stability*, Paris, 1962.

OECD; *The Problems of Profits and Other Non-Wage Incomes*, Second Report on Policies for Price Stability, by Working Party No. 4, Economic Policy Committee, Paris, February 1964, reproduced in large part in *Trade Union Affairs*, Summer 1964.

Oertzen, Peter von; *Betriebsräte in der Novemberrevolution*, Düsseldorf, Droste Verlag, 1963.

Oertzen, Peter von; 'Wo steht der DGB?', *Arbeitshefte*, 20 February 1964.

One Year Later, an Assessment of the Nation's Response to the Crisis, Described by the National Advisory Commission on Civil Disorders, Washington, DC, Urban America Inc., and The Urban Coalition, 1969.

Oulès, Firmin; *Economic Planning and Democracy*, Harmondsworth, Middlesex, Penguin, 1966.

Pribićević, Branko; *The Shop Stewards' Movement and Workers' Control*, Oxford, Blackwell, 1959.

Public Expenditure in 1963–4 and 1967–8, London, HMSO, 1963 (Cmnd 2235).

Reddaway, W. B.; 'Rising Prices for Ever?', *Lloyds Bank Review*, July 1966.

Reid, G. L., and Robertson, D. J. (eds.); *Fringe Benefits, Labour Costs and Social Security*, London, George Allen & Unwin, 1965.

Report of the National Advisory Commission on Civil Disorders (Riot Commission *Report*), New York, Bantam Books, 1968.

Risse, Heinz Theo; 'Abhängigkeit und Freiheit', in Marianne Feuersenger (ed.), *Gibt es noch ein Proletariat?*, q.v.

Roberts, Benjamin Charles; *Trade Union Government and Administration in Great Britain*, London, London School of Economics, 1956.

Ross, Arthur M., and Hartman, Paul T.; *Changing Patterns of Industrial Conflict*, New York, London, John Wiley & Sons, 1960.

Rowthorne, Bob: 'The Trap of an Incomes Policy', *New Left Review*, November–December 1965.

Rutzick, Max A.; 'Worker Skills in Current Defense Employment', *Monthly Labor Review*, September 1967.

Ryle, Anthony; *Student Casualties*, London, Allen Lane The Penguin Press, 1969.

Schweitzer, Pierre-Paul; 'International Aspects of the Full Employment Economy', *International Financial News Service*, 20 May 1966.

Science and Public Affairs, Bulletin of the Atomic Scientists, monthly.

Scientific American, monthly.

Scott, Anthony; 'Transatlantic and North American International Migration', paper read to the International Economic Association Conference on Mutual Repercussions of North American and Western European Economic Policies, Algarve, Portugal, 28 August – 4 September 1969 (roneo).

Seale, Patrick, and McConville, Maureen; *French Revolution 1968*, London: William Heinemann; Harmondsworth, Middlesex, Penguin Books, 1968.

Seldon, Arthur; 'Which Way to Welfare?', *Lloyds Bank Review*, October 1966.

Servan-Schreiber, Jean-Jacques; *The American Challenge,* Harmondsworth, Middlesex, Penguin Books, 1969.

Shonfield, Andrew; *Modern Capitalism: The Changing Balance of Public and Private Power*, Oxford University Press for The Royal Institute of International Affairs, 1965.

'Social Security in Britain and Certain Other Countries', *National Institute Economic Review*, No. 33, August 1965.

Socialist Commentary; London, monthly.

Socialist Register; London. The Merlin Press, annual from 1964.

Socialist Union; *Twentieth Century Socialism*, Harmondsworth, Middlesex, Penguin, 1956.

Sociological Review; University of Keele, Staffs., quarterly.

Speier, Hans, and Davison, W. Phillips (eds.); *West German Leaderships and Foreign Policy*, Evanston, Ill., Row, Peterson & Co., 1957.

Sraffa, Piero; *The Production of Commodities by Means of Commodities*, Cambridge University Press, 1960.

Stone, Jeremy J.; *The Case Against Missile Defences*, London, The Institute for Strategic Studies, Adelphi Paper No. 47, April 1968.

Strachey, John; *Contemporary Capitalism*, London, Victor Gollancz, 1956.

Stubbing, Richard A.; 'Improving the Acquisition Process for High Risk Electronics Systems', *Congressional Record*, 7 February 1969.

Sturmthal, Adolf; *Workers' Councils*, Cambridge, Mass., Harvard University Press, 1964.

Sweezy, Paul M. (ed.); *Eugen von Böhm-Bawerk's 'Karl Marx and the Close of his System' and Rudolf Hilferding's 'Böhm-Bawerk's Criticisms of Marx'*. New York, Augustus M. Kelly, 1949.

Tribune; London, weekly.

Trade Union Affairs; London, occasional (six issues, Winter 1960–Summer 1964).

Trades Union Congress; *Trade Unionism, the evidence of the Trade Union Congress to the Royal Commission on Trade Unions and Employers' Association*, London, TUC, November 1966.

TUC Reports, Report of Proceedings at the Trades Union Congress, annual.

Turner, H. A.; *The Trend of Strikes*, Leeds, Leeds University Press, 1963.

Turner, H. A., and Zoetewij, H.; *Prices, Wages and Incomes Policies in Industrialized Market Economies*, Geneva, International Labour Office, 1966.

United Nations, *Economic and Social Consequences of Disarmament*, New York, 1962.

University of Oxford Institute of Statistics, *Studies in War Economics*, Oxford, Basil Blackwell, 1947.

US Congress, Senate Committee on the Armed Services, *Military Procurement Authorization, Fiscal Year 1964*, Washington, DC.

——; House Subcommittee of the Committee on Appropriations, *Department of Defence Appropriations for 1964*, Washington, DC.

US Senate Subcommittee on Disarmament; *US Armament and Disarmament Problems* (Hearings), Washington, DC, 1967.

US Senate Subcommittee on Employment and Manpower, *Full Employment*; *Proposals for a Comprehensive Employment and Manpower Policy in the US*, Washington, DC, 1963.

Vester, Michael; 'SPD und Arbeitnehmerpolitik – Zum Dortmunder Parteitag der SPD', *Arbeitshefte*, 15 July 1966.

Vincent, Jean-Marie; 'Blick auf die italienischen Gewerkschaften', *Arbeitshefte*, 1 July 1963.

Wedderburn, K. W.; *The Worker and the Law*, Harmondsworth, Middlesex, Penguin, 1965.

Week, The; London, weekly.

Weir, Stanley; *A New Era of Labour Revolt, On the Job v. Official Unions*, Berkeley, Calif., Independent Socialist Club, 1966 (cyclostyled).

York, Herbert F.; 'Military Technology and National Security', *Scientific American*, March 1968.

Index

More about Penguins and Pelicans

Penguinews, which appears every month, contains details of all the new books issued by Penguins as they are published. From time to time it is supplemented by *Penguins in Print*, which is a complete list of all books published by Penguins which are in print. (There are well over three thousand of these.)

A specimen copy of *Penguinews* will be sent to you free on request, and you can become a subscriber for the price of the postage. For a year's issues (including the complete lists) please send 4s. if you live in the United Kingdom, or 8s. if you live elsewhere. Just write to Dept EP, Penguin Books Ltd, Harmondsworth, Middlesex, enclosing a cheque or postal order, and your name will be added to the mailing list.

Some other books published by Penguins are described on the following pages.

Note: *Penguinews* and *Penguins in Print* are not available in the U.S.A. or Canada.

Britain and the World Economy

J. M. Livingstone

In the world's market-place every country keeps
a stall and every country goes shopping. The
result – in currency, credit, and kind – is a
network of transactions as intricate and alive as
a printed circuit.

Britain and the World Economy is a short,
readable survey of the part played by one country
in this world network. Britain, partly by necessity,
partly by choice, plays a variety of economic
roles in the world and J. M. Livingstone
emphasizes the country's growing dependence on
events abroad, in this examination of her
contributions as an international banker operating
the sterling system; as the leader of a still
powerful Commonwealth; as a force in a
revitalized Europe; as a world trader; and as
a 'have' with responsibilities towards the
'have-nots'.

The Consumer Society

A History of American Capitalism

Peter d'A. Jones

How did America get rich? How has wealth
affected her people and her culture? What is the
future of her economy likely to be? These are
some of the questions dealt with in this dynamic
survey of the economic, social and political
forces that have made America the richest
country the world has ever known.

Skilfully blending economic theory and narrative
history, the author explains those elements of
colonial society that formed the basis for the
country's economic growth, the factors which
allowed it to progress from an agricultural
economy to an industrial one from 1860 to
1920 and finally the emergence of today's
consumer capitalism. He stresses his view
throughout that social democracy, mobility and
opportunity are the historical foundations of
America's wealth, and argues that so long as the
American people preserve an open society their
wealth will continue to grow.